Daughters of the King
Bible Study Series
Choices of the Heart

A 10-Lesson Bible Study for Individuals and Groups

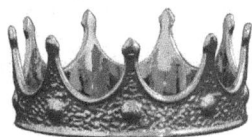

Endorsements

Choices of the Heart is an inspiring look at how famous and not-so-famous women of the Bible made choices in their lives. I had no idea that I could learn so much from the likes of Jezebel or Gomer. Kathy Collard Miller, in her gentle writing style, shows how these women and others, such as Deborah and Lydia, have made choices I often face. She sticks to the lives of these women from the Bible and brings the message home to the heart with thoughtful questions sprinkled throughout the text. *Choices* is a practical women's Bible study to learn how God uses all of our choices to honor him. Don't miss this opportunity to learn and grow from even the not-so-famous women of faith, who are like us.

—Susan K. Stewart,
Author, Speaker, Practical Inspirations

Kathy Collard Miller's *Choices of the Heart* is a Bible study full of sound scriptural principles, balanced spiritual wisdom, and a deep understanding of what matters most to women. Miller's study makes great use of an all-star, all female cast of leaders falling on both sides of the spiritual and moral equation. Her insightful questions invite the reader to reflect on her own life within a scriptural framework—prompting growth from the heart. I can't wait to use *Choices of the Heart* with my own women's bible study. I'm looking forward to more from Kathy Collard Miller!

—Catherine Finger,
EdD, Superintendent, Grayslake District 127, Grayslake, IL,
Speaker and Author of the *Murder with a Message* series.

Kathy Collard Miller

With each lesson, I was invited to recognize that choices of the heart aren't simple or defined without the grace of God. Each account of women in the Bible in this Bible study lifts a layer of possible misconception, asserts refreshing challenges, and presents applications of God's Word, bold yet gentle. At times, the reader is tugged to examine the heart and analyze motives. But with each lesson, the exhortation is profoundly clear, leaving a pleasant reassurance that we women today do have much in common with women of the Bible. Yet, we are called to learn from their examples to make godly choices as daughters of the King who dance to the melody of his redeeming love.

—**Janet Perez Eckles**,
author of *Simply Salsa: Dancing Without Fear at God's Fiesta*

Choices of the Heart from bestselling author Kathy Collard Miller is a must-read for all women who desire to walk in God's light as they become more like Jesus. This is not only a well-written book, but it is also laid out in such a way that it can be used by both individuals and groups. Highly recommended!

—**Kathi Macias**,
Multi-award-winning author of more than 50 books, including
The Singing Quilt and *Return to Christmas*.

Kathy Collard Miller thoughtfully addresses choices and attitudes that undermine or set us free. With encouragement and warmth, she helps us choose God's way and blessing. This exploration of biblical lives and choices can change your life.

—**Judith Couchman**,
Author of *Designing a Woman's Life* book, Bible study, and seminar

As the founder of Modern Day Princess Ministries, I am always looking to recommend resources for women that further the depth of our walk with Christ. The Daughter of the King series by Kathy Collard Miller does exactly that. It enables you to discover the wealth you have in knowing the King of Kings as your Heavenly Father and begin walking in the royalty you possess.

—**Doreen Hanna**,
Treasured Celebrations, Founder & President

Choices of the Heart provides excellent insight and instruction for the Christian woman who longs for more of God's Word. The women of the Bible come alive as they tackle life issues and struggles that are relevant to today's world. Kathy Collard Miller is a name you can trust for great Bible teaching.

—**Laura Petherbridge**,
Speaker and author of *The Smart Stepmom*,
101 Tips for The Smart Stepmom, and *When I Do Becomes I Don't—*
Practical Steps for Healing During Separation and Divorce

Kathy Collard Miller's new study, *Choices of the Heart*, gives us a treasure chest of encouragement and wisdom for a glorious life. Whether we struggle with the grittiness of jealousy, temptation or unforgiveness, Kathy points us to God who always gives us the power to move us into a meaningful pathway. I love the way Kathy takes the participant through the journey of examining the lives of women in the Bible and revealing the outcome of their bad and wise choices.

This is a great study for personal reflection during a devotion time or for discussions in a larger group setting. Kathy has done stellar research and written a masterpiece crafted to enrich the reader's knowledge of the Bible and their spiritual life.

—**Heidi McLaughlin**,
International speaker and author of
Sand to Pearls, Beauty Unleashed and *Restless for More*

Kathy Collard Miller

At the crux of every circumstance, we have two basic choices: whether to trust and whether to obey—intentional decisions to yield to God and embrace his Word. Kathy captures this powerful truth in *Choices of the Heart*. She invites us to walk with God in the great adventure of life, encouraged along the journey by our Heavenly Father's love and faithfulness. Such a motivating study!

—**Dawn Wilson**,
Founder of Heart Choices Today, San Diego, California,
President of Network of Evangelical Women in Ministry (NEWIM)

Elk Lake Publishing

Daughters of the King Bible Study Series

Choices of the Heart

Copyright © 2016 by Kathy Collard Miller

Requests for information should be addressed to:

Elk Lake Publishing, Atlanta, GA 30024

ISBN-13 Number: 978-1-64949-229-6

Graphic Design: Anna M. O'Brien

Editors: Christy Callahan, Deb Haggerty

Published in Association with Suzy Q Inc.

Daughters of the King
Bible Study Series
Choices of the Heart

A 10-Lesson Bible Study for Individuals and Groups

Kathy Collard Miller

Dedication

I dedicate this Bible study to the precious friends in our
"Soul Sisters" group: Dana, Kat, Lynnette, Gayle, Kendra,
and Lainey. I'm so grateful for your hearts of seeking God and for
encouraging me to do the same.

I also dedicate this to the women who have attended my
Heart Change Retreat. I have been blessed by your sharing
and inspired to love God more by hearing of his work in your life.

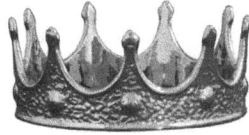

Table of Contents

Acknowledgments

Back in the 1990s, Mary Nelson of Accent Publications saw the potential of my idea for a Bible study series. With her guidance, the twelve-book study in the "Daughters of the King Bible Study Series" was created. I was grateful for her leadership.

Now I'm thrilled Fred St. Laurent and Deb Haggerty have understood and supported my vision of expanding the initial simple format to include commentary and greater depth. Thank you, Fred and Deb!

Christy Callahan has wisely edited my manuscript and made me look good. Great job, Christy! I appreciate you.

I'm always eager to acknowledge the love and support of my husband, Larry. Thank you, honey! You're the best.

Lesson 1

Rebekah and Rahab
Believing God's Sovereignty

Sometimes we wonder about God and the way he works. We begin to think we know better than he does, especially when he doesn't work in other people's lives the way we think he should. After all, change will be better for everyone!

Pastor and author Charles Swindoll defines God's sovereignty as "our all-wise, all-knowing God reigning in realms beyond our comprehension to bring about a plan beyond our ability to alter, hinder, or stop."[1] Thinking of Pastor Swindoll's definition makes us wonder why God doesn't just make the world a place where nothing bad happens. And, of course, the real question is, why do bad things happen to *me*?

But think for a moment what would happen if nothing challenging or bad occurred in your life. Would you need God? Would you grow emotionally or spiritually? Ask yourself, when have I been closer to God and become a better person? Usually, we come by such closeness

---

[1] Charles Swindoll, *Stones of Remembrance: Bible Study Guide* (Anaheim, CA: Insight for Living, 1988), 5.

while we are in the midst of difficult circumstances. Of course, not always but usually, if we seek God, we sense his love and care. Because of God's sovereignty, he allows difficult circumstances and situations in our lives. If we can see all things as being allowed by him, we will cooperate with his plan.

- How do you define good choices and bad choices?
  - o What influences your choices?
  - o How do you feel when someone doesn't make the choice you think they should?

Our reaction to what happens around us can give us a clue as to whether we're trusting God. If we're feeling tense or angry or reacting with control and manipulation, we might want to ask, *Do I really trust God's sovereignty? Do I truly believe God is loving and good?*

Rebekah and Rahab faced challenges and responded in different ways. The examples of their choices can help us recognize more of God's sovereignty—his ability to make his plan happen so he'll reveal his love and power. As a result, we'll increase our trust in him.

Rebekah

Rebekah is the wife of Isaac and the mother of twin sons, Esau and Jacob. She doesn't seem to have a sense at all of God's sovereignty and power. She takes matters into her own hands. Unfortunately, such control doesn't bring her the results she wants.

- Scan through Genesis 25:23, 27-34; 27:1-28:5. As the older son, Esau should receive the inheritance according to custom. What had God determined would happen between the twins (25:23)?
  o From Genesis 25:27-34, summarize what you observe about this

family's relationships and dynamics.

o Can you identify any of those same dynamics occurring in your family or relationships?

Sometimes God seems contradictory. After all, didn't he set up the rule stating the older son should receive the inheritance and the younger one be subservient? Yet, here he is commanding something different.

That's because God has a bigger plan. As he predicted, Esau and Jacob become the beginning of two nations still at odds today: the Israelites and the Arabs (originally the Edomites). When Esau and Jacob were born, no one could envision the future, yet God knew the result.

The amazing thing about God's sovereignty is how he fulfills his plans and predictions and yet, people have a free will to make their own choices. And somehow, those choices are incorporated into God's plan—a paradox stumping theologians even today.

Yes, God seems contradictory at times, but he knows the plans he has for our good and his glory (Jeremiah 29:11 and Romans 8:28). Let's see how Rebekah responds to God's "contradiction."

- What does Rebekah overhear (Genesis 27:1-5)?
- What wrong method(s) does she use to try to fulfill God's plan herself (vv. 6-10)?
  o Instead of her deceit, what godly reaction(s) could she have taken?

Rebekah decides to correct the situation herself instead of trusting in God's sovereignty and power. God had promised the elder son's blessing would go to Jacob, but she had no confidence in God's power to override Isaac's poor choice.

Can you think of a time when you saw someone making a poor choice and felt compelled to step in to steer the situation in a seemingly "better" way, yet you didn't seek God's will? Or you didn't take action, but your emotional response lacked grace and goodness? Now looking back, were you really trusting in God's sovereignty?

Think of other incidents where you are successful. A friend treats you with contempt, and you respond with grace. A child is disobedient, and you see how God disciplines you with patience. A family member disappoints you, and you offer the forgiveness God has given you. Someone gossips about you, and you remind yourself your value isn't in their opinion but in God's view of you.

In those times of failed or successful responses, think through what was going on within you. Did you reject or depend upon any Scripture? Did you recall any previous experience(s) contributing to your typical responses? What qualities of God did you cast away or rehearse?

These kinds of questions help us get in touch with our motives. They also help us be honest with our failures and successes rather than excusing ourselves or becoming proud.

- What are Jacob's misgivings about his mother's plan (Genesis 27:11-12)?
  o How does Rebekah respond to his fears (v. 13)?

So often, when we do something to try to make life better like Rebekah, we are actually making things worse. Rebekah thinks she is loving her beloved son, Jacob, "well." She thinks she is doing something to make his life better. She thinks she is protecting him from being abused and from injustice. And certainly, at times God will call us to protect and provide for people. But Rebekah isn't responding in God's power or in obedience to him. She never gives God a chance to correct the situation. She takes control herself.

Notice Jacob's fear. What is Rebekah teaching him about God and the way to deal with tension and injustice? Certainly not to trust God. She doesn't pray or instruct Jacob on "how to deal with disobedient people in a godly way." She doesn't model the way to communicate because she never tries to talk to her husband (as far as we know). Instead, she gives her son the example of deception and distrust.

Yet if someone had asked her whether she loved Jacob and wanted the best for him, she most likely would have answered, *Well, of course. Why else would I be doing this?*

We also are not loving someone "well" when we rescue them from experiencing God's discipline through the consequences of their poor behavior. We're also not loving them in a godly way when we don't trust God. We're encouraging them to distrust him also.

- Rebekah goes to a lot of trouble in her deception. What is the plan, and how does her plan turn out (Genesis 27:14-40)?
- How would you describe Rebekah's character at this point? What kind of woman is she?
- What is one of the results of her plan (v. 41)?
- What is another of the consequences (Genesis 27:42-28:5)?
- From Genesis 26:34-35 and 28:6-9, what aggravation filled her life?

If we could talk to Rebekah today, I'm sure she would defend her actions and sound convincing. She might say, *I'm only helping God fulfill his own plan. God promised Jacob would be the recipient of the inheritance, and I'm only helping to fulfill the promise. If I need to use a little deception to make sure my son gets what he deserves, then, well, the end justifies the means.*

Criticizing Rebekah in hindsight is easy. But don't you and I also rationalize at times with the "end justifies the means" excuse? We can convince ourselves we're merely claiming God's promise and assisting the fulfillment of his promise.

How can we protect ourselves from falling into this self-deceptive trap? We must seek the godly wisdom and guidance of others to get an objective perspective. Rebekah could have taken into account her son's reaction of fear to give her a clue as to what was happening. And she could have talked the situation over with her husband and trusted in the shield her submission would have been for her.

We can also pay attention to our inner compulsions. If we feel tense thinking of doing something, maybe we're forcing our way. Depending upon God and walking in righteousness produces peace (Isaiah 26:3). If we are not experiencing peace, we may be taking matters into our own hands rather than waiting upon God's timing and incorporating his methods.

Rebekah paid dearly for her distrust of God's sovereignty. She didn't realize Jacob's escape wouldn't be for just "a few days." Instead, she never saw her favorite son again and died before Jacob returned many years later. And in the meantime, she found life almost intolerable because of her pagan daughters-in-law.

The consequences of distrusting God's sovereignty were serious and significant in Rebekah's life. God gives us her example as a warning.

Rahab

In contrast to Rebekah, Rahab cooperates with God's sovereignty. As a result, his sovereign hand is revealed in many ways. She is an example of a pagan woman who puts her life in danger to follow God. Her story is profoundly revealing of how deep our trust can be. God divinely juxtaposes two spies to find a woman who has never walked in God's ways. He sovereignly knows she will be willing to sacrifice everything in order to respond to him.

Try to enter into her dangerous circumstances even though you may know the end of the story. She didn't know how her situation would end. Yet, she trusted in God's sovereign hand, which was revealed little by little.

You don't know the "end" of the story you're living, but in his sovereignty, God does. You can live in trust and faith knowing he will reveal his plan and purpose for you little by little.

- Read Joshua 2:1-24, 6:22-25. The Israelites are getting ready to move into Canaan, the Promised Land. Jericho is the first city they must conquer. Joshua sends two spies to check out the city. How are they protected (2:1-7 cf. 1:1-9)?
- What is Rahab's occupation (2:1)?

One of the mysteries of this story is how the Bible doesn't tell us how or why the two spies stay with Rahab. But author and speaker Liz Curtis Higgs has an interesting thought. "Where better to lie low than in a place with lots of traffic, where questions weren't asked, and strangers came and went at all hours? *Perfect.*"[2]

The most important thing to remember about this mystery is God responded to the fledgling belief of a woman who needed him desperately: a sinner needing a Savior God. We should feel more secure knowing no sin is too big for God's saving grace—even the sins of a prostitute running her own home business.

---

[2] Liz Curtis Higgs, *Bad Girls of the Bible: And What We Can Learn from Them* (Colorado Springs, CO: WaterBrook Press, 1999), 157.

- Rahab lies to protect the spies (Joshua 2:4-6). In your opinion, is lying ever justified?
  o If so, under what conditions?
  o If not, why not?

The Israelites were camping nearby, only about seven miles away. The spies would have stood out—their clothes must have been different. They had just crossed the Jordan River—maybe their clothes were still wet!

Everyone in town was talking about the threat. Rahab was smart to hide the men under the flax on the roof, because flax, when cut in the fields, is three to four feet high—easily high enough to cover the spies. After being cut down, flax is soaked in water for three to four weeks to separate the fibers. Then the fibers are dried in the sun on the roof before being spun into linen thread used for making clothing. Evidently, Rahab was an industrious entrepreneur with several businesses! Yet her dependence upon herself and her success did not prevent her from seeing God's sovereign hand in the arrival of the Israelites.

But the big question of the hour is, did Rahab do the right thing lying about hiding the spies? The Bible doesn't comment. We must remember she didn't yet know the God who forbids lying. More significantly, she risked her life to hide these strangers without any assurance she would gain anything. Talk about a woman of faith. God had planted faith within her based on the comments about the Israelites she'd heard from travelers. She knew the Israelites were going to be successful and, if she didn't jump on their bandwagon, she would be destroyed like the rest of her people.

Although none of her fellow citizens responded in faith, Rahab did—as well as her family, because of her "testimony."

- Fear for her life may have been Rahab's initial motivation for her faith in God. What other evidence do you see of her developing faith (Joshua 2:9-13)?
  o Considering her past, why is this such a big step for her?
  o Why is her plan dangerous?
  o What do you think gives her the courage to carry out her plan?

Rahab is acting with great courage because if she and the spies are caught, the spies might squeal on her under pressure. She is putting her whole being—and most likely her family's—into the care of men based solely on a blossoming faith in their God. This is one gutsy lady!

All the inhabitants of Jericho hear the news of what God has done through the Israelites, like part the Red Sea, yet only Rahab responds with faith in Jehovah, the Lord.

- If you had walked through Jericho, which person would you have identified as a likely candidate for faith?

Most likely not a sinful woman such as Rahab. Yet, she is the one who did respond to "rumors" about God's actions. God went to a great deal of trouble to bring her into the fold. His sovereign, gracious hand orchestrated everything needed to bring the truth to this needy and sinful woman.

- What plan do Rahab and the spies create (Joshua 2:15-24)?

This passage contains another clue as to why the spies could have easily found Rahab's home. She lived on the wall of the city, an easy place from which to quickly reach the gates if they were discovered before they found safety. Jericho, like many ancient fortified cities, had two walls built twelve to fifteen feet apart. Wooden planks covered the divide, and a house was built on top of the wood. Windows in the house would be available to look beyond the city walls.

Out of this window, Rahab placed the wonderful and saving scarlet cord to let the returning Israelites know which house was hers and to save herself and her family. Rahab's scarlet thread signifies the Holy Spirit in our lives. Through the Spirit, who is our "seal" (Ephesians 1:14), he assures us of salvation and reminds us we are one of God's forever princesses.

Many women are concerned about sins they committed before coming to know Christ, along with the sins they continue to struggle with. They wonder, *Can God forgive and cleanse me from such wrong things? Can I be secure in Christ?* Yes! A resounding yes! Because all sins are equal in God's eyes, and he provided salvation for every one of them: past, present, and future.

On a geographical note, within a half mile west of ancient Jericho are limestone cliffs about fifteen hundred feet in height. These cliffs contain many caves where Rahab likely directed the spies to hide.

- A cord of scarlet thread is Rahab's security (Joshua 2:18). What are the sources of security in various areas of your life?

We can imagine Rahab's worry as she wonders how everything will turn out. But she may have stared at the scarlet thread to fight against worry. The scarlet cord had to bring her and her family peace, reminding them they were safe and secure. Seeing the cord reminded them of God's sovereign dealings with them and gave them security, knowing if he did so much to reveal himself, he would keep his promise of deliverance.

There are many things in life we can depend upon for security. But they may not be related to dependence upon God's view of us as a member of God's family. Rahab could have depended upon money to bribe the spies to let her live. Rahab could have depended upon beauty to divert the spies' attention. Rahab could have depended upon intellect to convince the spies to save her life.

Those are temptations you and I could face today. But, just as Rahab depends upon her belief in God's protection, we can too. We can seek God's approval and not what society offers.

- Look at Joshua 6:22-25. The Israelites have defeated Jericho. What happens to Rahab and her family?

Although the spies aren't named in the biblical account (Joshua 2:1), one of them may have been Salmon. Why? Because Rahab marries him later (Matthew 1:5). At least our romantic hearts would like to think of love at first sight—even in a brothel! What an example of God's sovereign hand accomplishing something unusual to show his might and power.

- If faith gets us into God's kingdom, and what we do ("works") is the evidence of our faith (Ephesians 2:8-10; James 2:14-26), how do you need to strengthen each of these areas?
- How do you express each now?

Rahab not only had faith in God's sovereignty — she took action. Our salvation isn't dependent upon our works (Titus 3:5), because trusting him is a gift from God. We say to God, "I acknowledge I deserve to be on the cross because of my sins. But I believe you provided the substitute of Jesus so I can be cleansed and forgiven. I receive his death on my account. Now having you as my Lord and Savior, I can walk in your power on this earth."

What freedom we have to represent the Lord through the opportunities he gives us and to know he is transforming us more and more into the image of Jesus. Of course, Rahab didn't know all she was "signing up" for in joining the Israelite camp and taking on a relationship with Jehovah God. And neither do we when we first receive Christ as our Lord and Savior. But Rahab learns and becomes Salmon's wife. And so do we day by day and step by step. Our faith bears the fruit of action in obeying God and learning more and more about Him.

- Read Hebrews 11:11, 31. Rahab and Sarah are the only women mentioned by name in the Hebrews "Hall of Faith" passage. Why do you think God included them?
  o For what characteristics would God include you?
  o In what ways would you like your faith to grow?
- Rebekah tried to force God's plan to happen her own way, whereas Rahab cooperated with God's plan. What can you learn from each of them to help your trust in God grow, especially regarding the choices you make?

Isn't God gracious to provide biblical examples of those who made good choices and those who didn't? We have both in the stories of Rebekah and Rahab. God's sovereign touch is upon these women's lives, yet they had a choice whether to recognize his work and how they would respond.

God's control and power are surrounding every one of us, but we must look for his handiwork and then decide how we'll respond. We can take Rahab as our mentor for opening our eyes to God's work and will. And we will be blessed like she was.

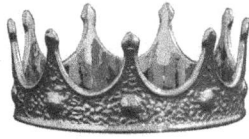

My precious Princess and Daughter:

I am in control. I am sovereign. I am able to make things happen the way I want. Yes, I do allow you to make your own choices. And I know you don't fully understand how these concepts can operate side by side. But I'm able to work within and around the choices you make to cause my ultimate purposes to succeed. For this, you must trust me. Ask me about your choices and plans. My wisdom is yours if you'll ask.

Just look at my Son's death and resurrection. His enemies thought they were acting on their own. Yet, while their choices revealed who they truly were, I made sure my words given to my prophets came true.

I want you to cooperate with my plans. When the people around you reject my leading, be assured, I am still in control. I will fulfill my plan. At times, I'll ask you to help me influence their lives, but don't take responsibility for them. Their choices are their own, but I'm still in control. Trust me. I'll use all things for your good.

Lovingly,

Your heavenly Father, the King

Lesson 2

Job's Wife and the Woman of Shunem
Trusting God's Goodness

We all wish only good things happened to us. But, alas! Life isn't that way. Every baby begins life with needs and sometimes pain. God implanted within us the drive to avoid being needy and avoid pain. He intended for that drive to motivate us to seek him, because ultimately he is the only one who can meet those needs and bring good out of pain. If we didn't have any needs or pain in this life, we wouldn't need an awareness of God's goodness. Nor would we try to depend upon God's goodness.

So in the midst of disappointments, trials, griefs, and any number of life's challenges, we search for relief but, often not with God's help. *No more bad stuff!* we cry, but those challenges keep coming. How are we to respond? How can we believe in God's goodness when life seems filled with so much pain?

If we're not experiencing difficulty or trials, we might not depend upon God because we think we deserve those privileges. After all, we've worked hard or been good or been generous. Any number of ideas could make us feel we've earned our status and comfort. And besides, how can God be good when he seems to bless some and not others?

- How do you define God's "goodness"?
  o How do you know when you're trusting God's goodness?
  o What is the worst thing you've ever been through?
  o How did you respond?

All women face challenges, especially trials questioning God's goodness. Let's learn from Job's wife and the woman of Shunem.

Job's Wife

If you relate to Job's wife's circumstances, which included wealth, ease, and success, you may take God's goodness for granted. After all, God has already taken care of you. You trust those provisions will never end and you could never be in danger. It would seem Job's wife had such an attitude.

But many other women aren't in her situation. They aren't comfortable financially or materially, and they may wonder whether God can ever provide. Or else they feel like God's goodness is just dripped out sparingly. Who knows? Maybe there was a time in Job's wife's life when she wasn't living in prosperity. At that time, her situation may have seemed hopeless, or she may have felt like her prayers for provision weren't being answered. Like us, she may have called out, "How is God good now?"

We can only guess about her past, but we can be assured we understand her current situation. Let's see what we can learn to avoid.

- Read Job 1:1-2:10. Based on the information given about Job's household, what kind of life did Job's wife enjoy before tragedy struck (1:1-5)?
- What do you learn about God's control over Satan's activities (vv. 6-12)?

Our beliefs about Satan can be hard to sort through. Different churches teach different things about Satan, his abilities, and God's restrictions upon him. There may not be clear answers to every question about him, but ultimately we know God reigns supreme (Revelation 20:1-10). Even when God allows Satan to tempt us, God is still good.

We also know from James 1:13-18 God tests but doesn't tempt us. He tests us to bring endurance (James 1:3), but our own selfish desires and motives tempt us for our destruction. Satan encourages that selfishness through circumstances and accusing thoughts (Revelation 12:10). Yet in the midst of all this, God wants us to know his goodness.

- Is it hard for you to comprehend or accept circumstances in which God allows tragedy? If so, can you explain why?
- What pain did Satan inflict on Job (Job 1:13-19, 2:7-8)?
  o What is Job's response to the disasters (1:20-22)?
- We see Job as the central character in this human drama, but each of these tragedies also touches Job's wife. What is her reaction (2:9)?
  o How would you describe Job's wife? Does any part of your description describe yourself?
  o Obviously, whatever belief she had in God's sovereignty and goodness had been destroyed by her circumstances. What circumstances tend to destroy your trust?

o Have there been times when you felt the same way as Job's wife? What were those circumstances?

o Do you think God was expecting too much from Job's wife to think she could cope with such tragedy?

Most women relate to Job's wife in some way, to some degree. None of us is exempt from trauma in some form. Regardless, we might be tempted to throw contempt upon her for her lack of faith in God's goodness. And at times, we may have criticized other women who have succumbed to doubt and distrust of God. But the truth is, any of us, regardless of the level of trust we think we have, could have times of extreme doubt. Let's be careful to have compassion for our sisters who are struggling. We may be there someday.

- Why do you think some people cope well with unhappy circumstances and other people do not?
- How does Job respond to his wife (Job 2:10)?
  o What sin does she commit and Job does not?
- If you were Job's wife, how would you have reacted to your husband?
  o When you're struggling with feelings of anger, depression, fear, pain, or hopelessness, how can people help you?
  o What response are you looking for when you tell people about your challenging situation?

We can give Job's wife some credit because she didn't immediately react with doubt. Like her, all of us have said discouraging things to others. We may have even had regrets afterward. *What was I thinking? How insensitive of me!* We react out of our own wrong beliefs, traumas, or pride. We can even think of ourselves as being very compassionate and then say something unwise or unloving. We wonder *Where did such words come from?*

But our words and actions reveal our hearts, and Job's wife's reaction is a warning for us. Although we know nothing about whether she cared for her heart—her spiritual life—and we know nothing about her commitment to Jehovah, we need to strengthen our hearts by being submerged in truth from Scripture, involving ourselves in Christian community for encouragement and being open to God's loving and good correction.

When we reveal our hearts in hurtful ways like Job's wife did, we don't need to be devastated and hopeless. We can go to God, asking for forgiveness and strengthening of our hearts. And if he directs, we need to confess and ask forgiveness of anyone we have hurt.

- What is Job's attitude about what happened to his wife and family (Job 1:20-21; 2:10)?
  o What is Job's attitude before tragedy strikes (1:1-5)?
  o What is your attitude or response when bad things happen to you and those you love?
  o What is your attitude or response when everything seems to be going well?

The Woman of Shunem

Now we turn to a woman whose belief in God's goodness was tested and, in the end, found trustworthy. No woman is faithful all the time and no woman fails in her trust in God's goodness all the time. We are always being tested and tempted so we can be stretched to have greater trust in God's goodness. And that strengthening, unfortunately, only comes through difficulty (James 1:2-4).

The words most used about this woman are "influential" and "wealthy." But her actions reveal important additional information. She is a strong woman who takes charge and action. God's Word focuses on her, thus her husband is a minor character.

- Read II Kings 4:8-37, 8:1-6. What kind of person is the woman of Shunem (4:8-13)?
  o How do her actions reveal her heart?
  o What do you like or dislike about her?
  o How are you similar to her and different from her?

Some women may relate to her strong personality and others may think she's too controlling. Regardless, God's Word portrays all kinds of people and shows their strengths *and* their weaknesses. Teaching us through people who experience victory and failure, the Bible can encourage us to know God cares about us and wants to be intimately involved in every person's life. And Jesus not only knows our "stories" but relates to our challenges, because he had a human body while on earth. In essence, he faced everything we face. Yet, he offers strength to us to be able to hold fast our faith (Hebrews 4:14-16) because he resisted every temptation.

This woman's hospitality was very common for Jewish culture but, evidently, no one else had offered this kind of help to Elisha. She steps up to the plate in helping Elisha. We can only imagine in what other ways she shared with others in her community or strangers passing through.

- Barrenness was the biggest disgrace in her culture. Why do you think the woman of Shunem is afraid to accept Elisha's promise (II Kings 4:16)?
- How do her fears come true (vv. 18-21)?

Because our desires at times seem so outrageous or even inappropriate, we may hesitate to even bring them before God's throne. Maybe we feel selfish. Maybe we can't believe God loves us *that* much. Maybe we wonder what others will think of us. We don't know this woman's motives, but we know the desire of her heart: a son! Having her desire fulfilled seems just too incredible. She doesn't want her hopes built up only to have them dashed to the ground.

- Why do you think the Shunammite woman doesn't tell her husband about their son's death and her purpose in going to Elisha (II Kings 4:22-24)?
  o Why do you think she doesn't tell Ghazi the purpose of her visit (v. 26)?
  o What do you think is going on in her mind when she replies, *"It is well"* (v. 26)?
  o Can you share a time when you were in horrible circumstances, but your soul could say *It is well*?

Shunem is a town in Galilee. The distance between where she lived and the edge of Mount Carmel is about fourteen or fifteen miles. She clearly believes only Elisha can give the answer to her secret desire.

Her husband's first response is *Why will you go to him today? It is neither new moon nor Sabbath* (v. 23). In other words, "Why would you want to go now? There's no religious reason." This could reveal she was in the habit of attending synagogue or religious services, possibly offered by Elisha. We see her heart for worshiping God.

- The woman of Shunem's grief is poured out before Elisha. How is her response different from the attitudes and responses of Job's wife (II Kings 4:28)?

- What does her idea of going to Elisha with her problem indicate about her spiritual perspective?
  o Why do you think she reacts the way she does?
  o Can you share a time when you had a similar response?
- Why do you think she isn't satisfied with Elisha sending Ghazi with his own staff as a possible healing measure (vv. 29-30)?
  o What does she want Elisha to do instead (v. 30)?

On the one hand, she seems to be surrendering to whatever God wants to do, but on the other hand, she's trying to run the show. We all can relate. We say we have faith in God's goodness and we believe God will do the right thing regardless, but our actions can reveal we think we know best.

- What is the end result of her actions (II Kings 4:31-37)?
  o How do you think she would have reacted if her son had not been restored to life?
- Look at II Kings 8:1-6. How does the woman of Shunem further show her reliance upon God (8:1-2)?
  o Why do you think her husband is not the recipient of Elisha's promises?
  o Why do you think we don't see him in this decision to move?

Some commentators believe the woman's husband has died. She is on her own now.

- How does God carefully arrange to restore the woman of Shunem with her rightful property (8:3-6)?
- Job's wife couldn't trust God's goodness, but the woman of

Shunem saw his goodness repeatedly even though unfortunate things happened to her. What would you like to change about your attitude toward God, people, and life when bad things happen?

o How could you focus more on God's goodness and sovereignty during those times?

• Read Jeremiah 29:11-13. Write a brief description of how these verses give you encouragement and faith during the hard times when God's goodness doesn't seem real.

One of the significant obstacles of trusting God's goodness is how we define "good." The world defines "good" circumstances as a lack of discomfort, struggle, doubt, and problems. God defines goodness differently. God is indeed good because he wants the best for everyone. But much of the time, he shows his goodness through difficulties, causing our hearts to depend upon him—which is the very best outcome.

Unfortunately, many people disagree. They ask, "If God is really loving and good, why would he allow evil in this world? Why do bad things happen?" Our explanation of how God uses everything for good (Romans 8:28) may not satisfy them because they don't want any challenges at all. But we can trust God truly knows what is best—for our good and for his glory.

As for Job's wife? There's every indication she stayed with her husband, because at the end of the story, more children are born to him. A different wife is not named.

And the woman of Shunem? She stayed faithful to Jehovah even when her prosperity and influence diminished. May we also continue to trust in God's goodness regardless of our circumstances.

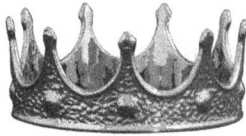

My precious Princess and Daughter:

I know your life has its ups and downs. I grieve with you when you mourn a loss, whether physical or emotional. I know you do not like the pain of unhappy times. On the surface, I may seem very unloving. I know your feelings. You don't need to hide them from me. I understand.

But can you trust me? I intend only good for you. I intend to bring flowers out of the ashes and joy out of the sadness. And if you're experiencing happiness right now, then enjoy! Don't feel guilty. I rejoice with you. I am blessed when you express your gratitude to me. I receive your love.

You see, I know the plans I have for you. I'm molding and refining your character so you can be a more useful vessel in my hands. Spiritual growth is how you'll find true fulfillment. I am eager to accomplish my plans in your life because you are my Daughter, my creation. I love and value you.

Lovingly,
Your heavenly Father, the King

Lesson 3

Jezebel and Deborah
Using Power and Influence

You have more power and influence than you think. Sometimes, since we are women, we think we don't have much. The world says it's a man's world. Even if that were true, God never intended things to be that way. Society has corrupted God's original plan, and today women feel like they need to fight to have power and influence.

People who don't know the Bible well can easily conclude the Bible is sexist, Jesus hated women and the apostle Paul wanted women to be treated as inferiors. But those are lies our enemy fosters.

Of course, we have roles God created and ordained, but in his plan there was never any intention of making roles about value or worth. God's words through Paul are *There is neither Jew nor Greek, there is neither slave nor free man, there is neither male nor female; for you are all one in Christ Jesus* (Galatians 3:28). What God did intend is as women are uniquely designed to value relationships (generally speaking), females hold great clout in making this world a better place—or a sadder one.

- Do you feel like you have very much influence upon others or in this world?
- In what ways have you impacted others?

In this lesson, we'll look at the lives of two biblical women who had tremendous leverage: Jezebel and Deborah. Both had great power, but Jezebel's impact was a negative, evil one, and Deborah's was positive and godly. Let's see what we can glean from their stories.

Jezebel

Jezebel is the daughter of parents from the country of Sidon and, therefore, not Hebrew and not raised to worship Jehovah. Her parents are worshipers of Baal, and so is she. Right from the beginning of this story, we see an example of influence: Jezebel's parents, whose influence ended up bringing untold grief to the people of Israel.

- Read I Kings 16:29-33, 18:4, 19:1-3; II Kings 9:30-37. What comparison does the biblical writer make about Ahab's choices?
- What was the first influence Jezebel had upon someone (I Kings 16:29-33)?
- Jezebel reigned with King Ahab during the time when God's prophet Elijah served the Israelites. There were many prophets of God then. What happened to many of them (18:4)?
  o What influence did Jezebel even wield over a godly man like Elijah (19:1-3)?
- Look at I Kings 21. What was the result of Jezebel's evil influence?
  o What godly choices could she have made instead?

Naboth the Jezreelite had every right and reason to refuse the king's request, which turns into a threat. The land belongs to Naboth's family and, in Israel, you are supposed to keep land in the family's possession unless you are so poor you have to sell your property. Then, the land would be returned to the family in the year of Jubilee. Obviously, Naboth isn't poor, and he doesn't need or want to sell his property. Instead, he values his land enough to keep it in the family.

Jezebel's concern over her husband might seem positive, but she quickly turns care into an evil scheme. Sometimes, our love for someone can turn ugly when we think we're loving them "well," but we're not motivated by righteousness. Of course, Jezebel has no regard for the laws and customs of Israel as a foreigner. And she only values her own life and those she cares about.

No wonder Ahab is so enamored with his wife. And no wonder she is maliciously motivated to please her husband. She'll do anything to make him happy, even break the law, to keep his admiration of her. Unfortunately, she has a built-in sense of power and selfishness, because she was raised in an ungodly home in Sidon—which doesn't excuse her sin. God holds everyone responsible for his or her own choices.

- How would you describe the emotional well-being and happiness in a woman like Jezebel?
  o In people today who use their influence for evil, what do you think motivates them to act in that way?
- How does Jezebel's influence affect the people around her?
- Why do you think God permitted Jezebel's evil influence to continue?
  o What is God's judgment upon Jezebel (I Kings 21:23)?
  o Why do you think God did this?
- What change of heart does Ahab have (v. 27)?

o How does God respond to Ahab's repentance (v. 29)?

o Do you think God would have responded similarly to Jezebel if she had repented?

We're shocked, maybe even frustrated, when God pardons such wickedness. We might believe there should be a limit to what he can forgive. God was indicating even then the degree of his grace which would later be fully revealed through Jesus. Jesus died on the cross for each and every one of our transgressions, regardless of how evil the sin.

And, in fact, we all stand at the cross on equal ground. There is no grading of sin. Even the worst murderer can be forgiven and cleansed and receive new life because of God's grace, which is never earned or deserved. And our forgiven sins qualify us to be used by God for a godly influence. The good news of the gospel includes God's purposes for us.

Repentance will bring new life, but the results of sin may still occur. God is merciful in delaying his punishment of Ahab, but Ahab still suffers some consequences (I Kings 21:29; 22:34-38, 51-53). What does this tell you about the effects of his sin?

- How is God's prophecy about Jezebel fulfilled (II Kings 9:30-37)?
  o Though God's judgment seems to be delayed at times, what always happens as a result of sinful choices and a sinful lifestyle?
- What should our attitude be as we observe the evildoing of ungodly people (Psalm 37:1-10)?

Deborah

The prophetess Deborah serves as a wonderful example of godliness and right worship of Jehovah. Interestingly, Deborah lived before Jezebel and, if Jezebel had cared to learn and take to heart the godly examples from Israel's history, she could have learned what a godly woman can be who has powerful influence. Or maybe she did know about Deborah but freely chose the opposite. We don't know Jezebel's motives, other than wanting to have her needs met. With Deborah, we can easily see her motives of wanting to glorify God and serve the people righteously.

Deborah was chosen by God to settle disputes, point out ungodly actions in others and correct spiritual errors. She also gives messages from God as his Spirit enlightens her. Her name means "bee," and obviously she is as industrious and effective as the bees in any beehive.

- Read Judges 4 and 5. What were the circumstances in Israel at the time Deborah lived (4:1-3)?

Israel has been experiencing eighty years of rest and prosperity. Unfortunately, with prosperity comes a sense of entitlement, a sense of deserving favor rather than viewing their peaceable season as God's unconditional favor.

This cycle occurred often in Israel's history. When they are in distress, they are motivated to call upon God for his help and deliverance. But then, after he gives prosperity and security, they take his blessing for granted and turn away from him.

Some of us can experience the same kind of destructive cycle if we're not careful to remain faithful in our walk with God.

- What do we learn about the leadership of Deborah (Judges 4:4-6)?
  o What does Deborah's position as a judge of Israel indicate about God? If meaningful for you, explain.

Deborah is the fourth judge of Israel and the only female. Obviously God uses anyone who is dedicated to serving him, male or female. She doesn't seek out power but follows God's directions when called upon. She's also so focused on God's glory that she easily delegates responsibility, trusting God to empower others, even if they don't perform the way she would prefer or think best.

- Which of Deborah's qualities enabled her to lead a nation, go out to battle, and influence others to obey God (Judges 4:6-10)?

  o What was wrong with Barak's attitude (vv. 8-10)?

  o To what do you attribute Deborah's bold confidence (v. 14)?

- What characteristics of Deborah's would you like to develop in your life? Why?

- With Deborah's great influence and success, she could have become proud, but instead, she gives God the glory and credit (5:1-5). What have you found helpful in keeping a humble attitude, especially after experiencing power and success?

  o In verse 7, Deborah does give herself some credit. How can humility and giving ourselves deserved credit fit together?

  o How does Deborah's praise of Jael further show her leadership abilities and humility (4:15-24, 5:24-27)?

Music and praising God in song had always been an important and valued part of Jewish life and history. There's every possibility this victory praise song was created by Deborah and Barak. Such songs function as both praising God and recording God's work. Most of us can memorize and remember lyrics better than just words.

Music and lyrics were also God's way of reminding the Israelites of God's faithfulness and his principles. Children could participate and learn about God through songs before they ever learn the details of Hebrew. God used music in many different ways, and Deborah valued such worship.

Below is a list of leadership qualities. Using a number between one and five, indicate your level of improvement needed. (One equals little improvement needed. Five equals great improvement needed). Also, indicate how you think you could improve the quality.

Quality	Number & How to Improve
Patience	
Gentleness	
Communication skills	
Listening skills	
Giving unconditional love	
Following through on promises	
Establishing correct priorities	
Forgiving	
Affirming others	
Godly assertiveness	

- What other qualities would you see as important leadership characteristics?

How would you compare and contrast Jezebel's leadership with Deborah's?

	Jezebel & Deborah
Similarities	
Differences	

- What situations or circumstances do you anticipate facing this week where you could focus greater attention on one quality you want to improve?
- What effect do the following choices have on being a godly influence? How do they diminish a Christ-like attitude?
  o gossip:
  o self-centeredness:
  o bitterness:
  o backbiting:
  o unrealistic expectations:
  o anger:
  o covetousness:
  o pride:
  o harshness:
- In what ways do you consider yourself influential (possible areas: witnessing, family, hospitality, career, community involvement, ministering to other Christians, etc.)?

Although no one wakes up planning to be like Jezebel, we've all at some point influenced or attacked others in unfortunate ways, sometimes without intending to do so. We can carry bitterness toward someone who has hurt us and such anger diminishes our power to be an influencer for God. If we neglect spiritual disciplines like Bible study, prayer, Scripture memorization, and meditation, we will lack knowledge and confidence in how God wants to lead us, and to lead others through us.

We may want to be like Deborah, but unless we intentionally nurture our spiritual life, we could end up like Jezebel. Let's be alert to God's invitations to be influential for him in righteousness.

My precious Princess and Daughter:

I'm excited about using your influence on others. Your society may try to convince you you're insignificant and powerless, but I can empower you to make a difference. You were created with a purpose, and I know exactly what I want to accomplish through you.

At times, you may think what I'm calling you to isn't significant. Many of my callings are not valued by the world. Diapering a baby may not seem influential. Helping at a shelter may not seem significant. But anything I call you to is significant in my eyes. So agree with what I find important and respond to my call regardless of the world's values.

I understand your broken heart when it seems you've failed. You may believe you've touched others in a hurtful way. But I am powerful enough to correct and heal even sin. Will you confess those areas of failure or disobedience? I'll forgive you—and help you to forgive others and for them to forgive you. Do all you can in my power and continue growing in love toward others. You are making progress. I'm pleased.

Lovingly,

Your heavenly Father, the King

Lesson 4

Naomi and the Syrophoenician Woman
Praying Powerfully

At times, we wonder whether our prayers are going any higher than the ceiling of our homes, the roofs of our cars or the top floor of our office building. We plead, beg, claim Scripture, glean from books on prayer and ask others to pray.

We want to have intimacy with God through prayer, yet often our hearts feel as cold as a marble floor in winter. When we're bowled over by some problem, God may not immediately answer our pleas, and we wonder why. Doesn't God promise he will answer our prayers if we ask?

Unfortunately, when those prayers don't get answered at all, or the answer isn't what we asked for, we can easily conclude God doesn't care, doesn't love us, isn't good, or he must be helpless. We hate those doubts, but they seem to assail us.

- When your prayers aren't answered right away, how do you feel?
  o Can you think of anything positive resulting from a delay, an unwanted answer, or a no to one of your prayers?

Naomi and the Syrophoenician woman may have experienced such feelings. But God intervened in his timing and method. We can glean much from them about the power of prayer. Maybe their light can chase away some of the shadows in our prayer closets.

Naomi

Naomi is a wife whose husband, Elimelech, decides to deal with the famine by moving to a non-Hebrew land. Moab is about fifty miles east of Israel on the other side of the Dead Sea—quite a trek to travel.

- Read the book of Ruth. What happened in Naomi's life to make her feel unloved by God and discouraged (1:1-5)?
  o Do you think she had prayed for these very kind of things not to happen?
  o If she had, how had God's no answer contributed to her mental state?
  o Do her feelings reflect her faith?
- God often answers prayer with one of three possible answers: no, yes, or wait. Which answer is most difficult for you?
- For each of them, write out two to three brief, personal examples of how God answered you in the past with:
  o Yes:
  o No:
  o Wait:

Elimelech may be credited with trying to provide for his family and, obviously, he heard or believed there wasn't any famine in Moab. Unfortunately, his choice reveals his lack of trust in God's provision. We don't know how many families left the area, but chances are some people who stayed must criticize those who left. Any who are following the Lord then believe the famine is a judgment from Jehovah and, if people would turn back to him, the famine would end. Elimelech most likely plans on staying in Moab until the end of the famine, but evidently doubts prosperity will happen soon enough before they starve.

Elimelech and Naomi's decision to leave is revealing, since many Hebrew people had adopted the worship of the Canaanite god Baal and believe God created the famine. Baal is believed to be the owner of the land and therefore responsible for what the crops produce. According to the pagan priests' teaching, Baal's female counterpart "god" is Asherah, and sexual intercourse between the two gods regulates crop success. When God "produces" a famine, he is showing he's in charge of the land and Baal and Asherah are not real. God clearly demonstrates he is the sovereign God, and he answers prayer. No matter how much the people worship the false gods through sacrificing to them, Baal and Asherah can't respond. Elimelech may have bought into the idea God is powerless to end the famine.

- Naomi must have represented God in positive ways because one daughter-in-law, Ruth, doesn't want to leave her. Even though God uses Naomi to influence others, what is Naomi's opinion of God's dealings with her (Ruth 1:19-21)?
  o Do you think Naomi prays regularly and worships God faithfully? Why or why not?
  o How could she keep a godly attitude?

After Naomi's husband and sons die, she hears there is now rain in Israel and crops are producing. We can only imagine her feelings, some glad, and some distressed. Is she thinking *What will it be like if I return? Will people criticize me? Are my old friends still alive? How can I make a living? I can't imagine my daughters-in-law wanting to come with me and they shouldn't. I haven't been a good representative of Jehovah.*

We have to wonder how much Naomi, Elimelech, and their sons spoke to the two girls about Jehovah since they haven't become converts.

- Although our feelings may not always be pleasant, we can still tell ourselves the truth with our minds. Evidently, Naomi has convinced herself God is against her. What is actually the truth?

We don't know how Naomi feels about her husband's decision to escape to Moab, but her depression could stem partly from regret about cooperating with his ungodly decision. Or maybe she criticizes herself because she didn't encourage him to trust God. We'll never know, but those kinds of reactions can certainly occur within us and cause depression.

- At times a no answer makes us see God as not being loving, kind, wise, or powerful. How can we correct such an inaccurate view of God?
- Why does Naomi call herself Mara (Ruth 1:20)?
  o How can we prevent God's no answers from creating bitterness in our hearts?
  o Can you recount a time when you were tempted to become bitter? What happened?

Ironically, the name Naomi means "sweetness" or "pleasantness." Naomi was far from sweet or pleasant.

- Life begins to turn around for Naomi even though we have no record of her asking God to bring her blessings. What good things happen to her?
  o 1:22-2:6:
  o 2:19-23:
  o 3:16-18:
  o 4:9-12:
  o 4:13-17:

Ruth's decision to follow Naomi is significant, because she surrenders the possibility of ever marrying and having a child, which is the only way for a woman to be provided for in old age. She knows no Jewish man would want a non-Jewish wife. She is considered an "idolater" from another country, even if Naomi recommends her.

Ruth also choses to follow her mother-in-law, knowing Naomi isn't pleasant to be around. Just imagine for a moment the difficulty of being with a bitter, complaining woman who you feel responsible to provide for—and possibly even make happy—in a foreign land. Ruth really sacrifices a lot to throw her lot in with a new group of people. Maybe Naomi did something right in representing God.

- Matthew 1:5 tells us Naomi's grandson, Obed, is in the lineage of Jesus. What does this teach us about God's graciousness even when we feel discouraged or depressed about God's no answers?
- Just as God's control over the events in the book of Ruth is not specifically mentioned, there are no "coincidences" in the lives of Christians. What does Naomi's story and Ruth's part in the story show us about these "coincidences"?

The Syrophoenician Woman

The Syrophoenician woman truly represents a prayer warrior. Her need is dire for her and her daughter. What's amazing is she is a Gentile. In this account, Jesus goes to the region of Tyre and Sidon, on the Mediterranean coast. This is the only time Scripture indicates Jesus left the land of Israel. Just as he *had to go* through Samaria to meet the shunned woman at the well, so he must leave his country to meet this needy woman. How gracious of him!

- Read Matthew 15:21-28 and Mark 7:24-30. The Syrophoenician woman is not Jewish. She is Canaanite. In Matthew 15:22, how did she acknowledge her:
  o dependence upon Jesus:
  o belief in Jesus as God:

In Mark's gospel account, this woman is identified as a Greek, born in Syrian Phoencia. The cities of Sidon and Tyre are in that area, which is northwest of Galilee.

The apostle Matthew, when he writes his gospel, describes her as a Canaanite, which is true. But by using that word instead of something general like *Gentile*, he is emphasizing the significance of what Jesus does for her. She isn't just a Gentile, but comes from a long history of her people, the Canaanites, being despised by Jews.

The Canaanites of Jesus' day are descendants of the Canaanites in Joshua's day—the same people God had commanded to be wiped out. But, because of the disobedience of the Israelite invading army, some survived. Survivors like this Gentile woman are despised because they represent the Jewish race's history of disobedience. Plus, Canaanites are considered "unclean." There are many reasons this woman had no right or invitation to engage Rabbi Jesus. However, her desperation and her faith compelled her. We can only imagine how she originally heard about him.

- How is her faith in Jesus' power and omniscience shown in her words (Matthew 15:22)?

Here is a woman who boldly and bluntly gives Jesus her request. She doesn't even ask for something specific to be done. She just states her situation. This is as much prayer as the silent or spoken prayer request. She just approaches God and trusts in his goodness. At first, her faith is not appreciated. Jesus completely ignores her.

- How would Jesus' lack of response have made you feel if you were that woman?
  o What would you have done?
  o Do her actions surprise you?
  o How do you feel when God's answer is "wait" to your plea? Do you think he is ignoring your need?
- The disciples, typical Jews of that day, despise Gentiles like this woman. How could the prejudice of Jews account for the disciples' reaction to this woman (Matthew 15:23)?
  o Why else might the disciples have reacted unkindly toward the woman (v. 23)?
  o Do you think they were surprised when Jesus finally talked to the woman and eventually answered her request? Why?

This needy woman overcomes a huge obstacle to approaching Jesus. We need to remember she could have feared violence. She could have wondered if they would push her away physically. At the least, she must expect verbal abuse. She is not only a Gentile—she is female, and Jewish men don't even give respect to Jewish women.

We don't know how loud the disciples talk when they address Jesus, saying he should send her away. Does she hear them? If so, their comments must increase her fears. There is no support for her at all.

It's admirable that the disciples don't take any action without consulting him. But they have the boldness to tell Jesus what to do! In comparison, the woman has more trust in Jesus as she makes her request. She doesn't tell him what to do! She rests in believing he knows best.

Maybe this is not only a lesson in trust for the woman, but a teaching moment for his followers. Would they learn to give respect to everyone as their master did?

- In the conversation between Jesus and the woman in Matthew 15:24-27, what do you learn about:
  o Persistence in *prayer*:
  o Creativity in prayer:
  o Claiming God's promises:
  o Believing God's answers are best for you:
- Even though Jesus' answer seems cruel, what do you think he is actually trying to do? Could he be developing her faith and dependence upon him or something else?
  o Do you think he would respond in the same way when he deals with a less assertive person?

When Jesus uses the word "dog," he is referring to the Jewish practice of calling Gentiles "dogs," which is demeaning because dogs were known as unclean animals. Unlike our pets, dogs were far from favored. They roamed the streets eating anything they could find, including food no Jew would touch, much less eat.

Jews believed a Gentile wasn't entitled to receive God's blessing or be redeemed by the Messiah. Jesus knows he will shortly be blessing her, so he wants everyone to know, though they regard her as unworthy, he loves her and is wooing her into his kingdom. What a lesson for his disciples, who later will be called to reach out to everyone with the gospel—including Gentiles. They never would have believed their master would call them to do something so seemingly outrageously wrong.

To what degree this woman understands what's going on we don't know, but she is willing to be considered a "dog" in order to have her daughter healed—she doesn't refute that fact. She'll do anything to help her daughter, and she knows Jesus is her only hope.

- This woman cannot make her request as a member of the household of Israel. But on what basis does she make her request (Matthew 15:27)?
  - Do you feel at times as if you are living on the crumbs of faith and don't feel worthy or entitled to come to God with your praise or requests?
  - How does the Syrophoenician woman help you grow bolder in prayer during those times?
  - How long has it been since you approached God in awe-filled worship?
- What would you like to ask God for today? How does this Gentile woman encourage you to bring your requests to him?
- Why does Jesus grant her request (v. 28)?
  - What do you think her "great faith" refers to (v. 28)?
- If you had been that woman, would you have hesitated to leave Jesus' presence and go home to find out whether his promise had come true?

Kathy Collard Miller

o How does her leaving prove her faith even more?

- The next time God says wait in answer to your prayer, what lesson about the Syrophoenician woman will strengthen you?
- What guidelines for answered prayers do John 15:7 and John 16:24 give us?
  o What other guidelines about prayer from Scripture can you think of?

60

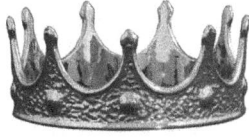

My precious Princess and Daughter:

Do you think I don't hear you? Do you think I sometimes ignore you? Do you feel misunderstood when I answer no? Can you believe I understand? I know you have a hard time trusting my answers all the time. Adam and Eve started this distrust of me. Satan is the father of all such lies. He hates me—and he is still trying to get my children to doubt me.

But remember, your vision is limited. I can see everything. You can't know what your desired answer might mean in the future. I already am in the future. You believe what you want is best. But I know best. My answer is always right and good. I respond with your best in mind. My plans are formed by my love.

So keep asking. I'm eager to hear you. I'm listening. Whether I answer yes, no, or wait—trust me.

Lovingly,

Your heavenly Father, the King

Lesson 5

Gomer and the Forgiven Woman Taking Hold of Forgiveness

Why is accepting God's forgiveness so hard for us at times? We may believe what we've done seems unforgivable. Or we may think we have to be sorry "enough." Sometimes we think the more repentant we are, the more we'll avoid repeating our offense. Or maybe we've asked so many times to be forgiven for the same thing we believe God has given up on us. We could easily imagine God standing up in heaven with his arms crossed in front of him, frowning and tapping his foot, saying, "I've forgiven you so many times. When are you going to get your act together? I only have so much grace after all."

But the wonderful and amazing thing is, God's grace is accompanied by his mercy which can be defined as "unlimited second chances." Oh, how we need many second chances. When we also keep in mind the fact God doesn't expect us to become perfect on this earth, we can have hope. And a large part of that hope is believing God wants to forgive the first time and then continually.

- Is accepting God's forgiveness difficult or easy for you?
  o Do you feel like you must somehow earn back God's favor? In what way?

Hope is what the stories of Gomer and the forgiven woman teach us. God reaches out again and again to woo us and actually already considers us perfect in his eyes (Colossians 1:10) as his princesses. And a part of our inheritance is forgiveness, both at the point of salvation and throughout our earthly existence. Let's see what these two biblical women offer us.

Gomer

Gomer represents Israel, who turns away from their Lord God time and time again. Hosea's response to her represents God's response to a sinning nation and is God's reassuring message he'll do the same with us. God wants Gomer (and Israel) to see herself through his own eyes: she is lovely and his love for her is not based upon her behavior. God knows her life will be better by staying faithful to her husband, because she will experience love, protection, and security. She'll be able to see herself as cleansed, valuable, and significant. If she doesn't stay faithful, his love for her never wavers or ends.

The same applies to us. God calls us to himself to enjoy his good gifts and to turn away from the destructive consequences of sin, which Jesus made possible by his death and resurrection.

- Read Hosea 1-3. Why does God command the prophet to marry Gomer and have children with her (1:1-11)?

Each of Hosea and Gomer's children's names mean something important. The first child is Jezreel, meaning "God will scatter," because Israel was about to be attacked by Assyria in the valley of Jezreel. The second child is Lo-Ruhamah, meaning "unpitied," because God's pity had ended. In an effort to bring Israel to repentance, the Israelites would be taken into captivity. And the third, Lo-Ammi, meaning "not my people," because God was not acknowledging these Israelites as his own people.

Although the names might seem to spell permanent rejection, if you read Hosea chapter 4-14 (even though we won't for this study), you'll see the disciplining he gives them is temporary. God continues to try to woo them to himself.

- When Gomer is acting in sin, what is Hosea's attitude toward her (2:1-13)?

It's difficult for us to understand all the symbolism in the book of Hosea. But keep in mind, Israel (represented by Gomer) is called a harlot, because the nation has put its affections—worship—toward other gods, making Jehovah like a jilted husband. Its "gods" are things like looking to other countries to provide and protect them. Thus, the Israelites show how they regard God as impotent and unloving, thus besmudging his name before other nations. They also offer sacrifices to the foreign "god," Baal. Although Israel keeps God's appointed religious holidays and services, their hearts aren't sincerely worshipping. Their "worship" is all for show in an attempt to get God to do what they want.

- What is the purpose of the discipline Hosea gives Gomer (Hosea 2:6-7)?
- How does Hosea try to woo Gomer back to him (vv. 14-15)?

- What does his loving heart represent to you about God wooing Israel and us back to himself?

The phrase "bring her into the wilderness" is describing how God will separate Israel from opportunities to worship other "loves." Sometimes God does the same thing with us. He puts obstacles in our way to help us stop sinning. For instance, we may feel depressed because we are making ungodly choices. Although depression can have a physical cause, God can use even overwhelming sadness to motivate us to call upon him to help us.

- What does Hosea/God plan to do when Gomer/Israel turns back to him (Hosea 2:21-23)?
- How does Hosea demonstrate his persistent love for Gomer (3:1-3)?
  o In what ways does this represent God's desire and willingness to forgive great and/or persistent sin?
- What is God confident Gomer/Israel will do (vv. 4-5)?

With most of these verses, Hosea is referring to the future experiences of the Israelites. He contrasts the present condition of Israel with their future in these ways:

- "Without a king": no royal family nor national control. Interestingly, the coregent gods Baal and Astarte are a kind of "royal couple" whom the Israelites worship. Hosea 3:1 refers to "raisin cakes," which are known to be offered in worship to Astarte. Evidently, they were offered to Baal as well.
- "Without sacrifice or pillar/stones": Levitical sacrifices have been temporarily stopped.

- "Without ephod or idols": methods of guidance. In this case, these refer to ungodly sources the Israelites have used.

- Have you ever experienced that kind of love and forgiveness? Describe briefly.
- If God expected Hosea to forgive such great sin in his wife, then how much forgiveness does he want us to have for others?
    o Is there anyone who has hurt you whom you haven't yet forgiven How would you characterize the kind of love Hosea has for Gomer, which represents God's kind of love toward his wayward children?
    o What do you think God wants you to do and why?

The Forgiven Woman

We don't know much about this woman. She is a known "sinner" in the community and is treated with contempt by everyone. She most likely was a prostitute, and the townspeople easily felt themselves above her. Unlike them, she wants to be forgiven. Jesus values her repentant and worshipful heart.

Jesus contrasts her to a man who considers himself "righteous." He believes he doesn't need forgiveness for anything because he has declared himself righteous. He is motivated by a need to be seen important. The Pharisee is proud and doesn't worship Jesus. He doesn't even provide the common courtesies like washing his guest's feet. Such a lack of hospitality would seem to show the Pharisee's subtle contempt of Jesus.

- Read Luke 7:36-50. What did this woman do for Jesus (vv. 36-38)?
- If you were that woman, what feelings would you experience?

o How great do you think her sin had been for her to act in this way?

Since this woman is an immoral woman, her perfume has probably been used for sensual purposes. Perfume is one of the tools of her trade. Alabaster jars are very expensive and have beautiful carvings on them. An expensive and beautiful jar could indicate the success and desirability of the woman in her business. We don't know the size or condition of this jar, but these jars are often small, allowing her to easily carry her *tool*. The perfume was so potent she could use a tiny bit to smell attractive. But by lavishing all the perfume on Jesus, she indicated her total dependence upon God's provision for the rest of her life.

- Why do you think Jesus has no trouble accepting a gift intended originally for evil?
- Why do you think Jesus willingly accepts a sinful life relinquished to his use?
- What is the Pharisee's reaction to this scene in his home (Luke 7:39)?
- How does this represent the opinions of many in the world today, sometimes even Christians?
- Jesus answers the Pharisee's thoughts. Would you have answered Jesus' question the same way as the Pharisee did (vv. 40-43)?
  o Does the Pharisee sound very convinced?
  o Why do you think he has reservations about his answer?
  o Have you ever felt like you wanted to do for Jesus what this woman did?
  o Were you more like the Pharisee or this woman when you welcomed Jesus into your heart and life (vv. 44-46)?

We need to fully appreciate the courage and brokenheartedness motivating this woman to risk so much. She might wonder how Jesus would respond to the overture of her heart. Of course, she doesn't actually join the men at the table because men didn't sit to eat. They reclined on the floor at a low table. Jesus' feet are extended outward from the table and easily accessible to her.

We might wonder why the Pharisee's servants didn't toss her out. The poor were allowed to come to such a public banquet to "glean" the leftovers. But, we have to wonder whether she felt comfortable entering the Pharisee's house because she had been there before on "business." Maybe the Pharisee's critical and contemptuous words were meant to intimidate the woman so not to bring accusations against his own sin. Many times, we criticize and pour contempt on others because we believe they're threatening us.

Even today many of those who don't follow Jesus criticize those who do, because followers of Christ demonstrate a certain peace and confidence, silently causing self-contempt within others' own unbelieving hearts. If someone is responding negatively to your godly behavior, don't blame yourself. Their reaction may not be so much about you as about their own guilty conscience.

- Have you ever personally experienced the truth of Luke 7, verse 47?
  o How do you think the woman felt when Jesus told her her sins were forgiven (v. 48)?
- Do you seek and receive God's forgiveness after each sin?
  o Are you a person who has been forgiven much or little?
  o Have you expressed your gratitude to God for his forgiveness? How do you say thank you?

Sometimes, we get in the habit of waiting until bedtime to ask Jesus to forgive us for all the sins we've done during the day, putting us at a disadvantage. We never lose our salvation by sinning, but sin separates us from fellowship with God and receiving his empowering. By asking for his forgiveness and cleansing immediately after each sin, we restore our fellowship and have his power available to resist the next temptation.

- Are you still begging for forgiveness at Jesus' feet about some sin when he has already forgiven you and said, "Go in peace"? If so, what do you think he wants you to do?

Sometimes, like the woman who was forgiven, we keep crying and begging for forgiveness at Jesus' feet when he wants us to acknowledge we are cleansed and our sin has been wiped away. He wants us to go in peace and stop rehearsing our sin. The Amplified Bible uses the words, *go in peace [free from the distress experienced as the result of sin]* (Luke 7:50).

- What was the woman's faith based on (Luke 7:45-50)?
- Read I John 1:9. What are the requirements for being forgiven?
  o Have you ever tried to add some act of penance onto that verse, like mentally beating yourself up? Describe.
  o What do you think Jesus wants your attitude to be now?

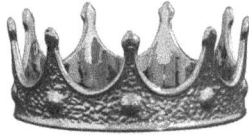

My precious Princess and Daughter:

How I long to forgive you. How I want to focus on your love for me, not your sin. Why do you keep reminding me of your failures when I've already forgotten? You can't forget, but I can wipe any wrongdoing from the slate, as if you've never sinned. Never! That's how much My forgiveness can mean to you. Receive my grace as your own.

You struggle to understand my forgiveness, but sin separates you from me, and I want to enjoy your fellowship. My Spirit is available within you to empower you, but unforgiven sin blocks that power. When you continue to beat yourself up, your focus is on yourself, not my loving forgiveness. Satan attempts to make you feel unworthy and unforgiven.

And when you feel ashamed, and you can't comprehend my loving desire to forgive you, just remember I enjoy your company. I forgive you because your fellowship is so important to me. In fact, restoring our fellowship is for my sake along with yours. Why do you think I created you? Although I don't need your company, I do enjoy your heart seeking me. Come to me and drink from my fountain of forgiveness and peace, which is flowing for you.

Lovingly,

Your heavenly Father, the King

Lesson 6

Sarah and Lydia
Obeying God's Plan

Obeying God and then seeing the good results is always a thrill. When we're hesitant to obey God, we wonder why. Well, the fact is there don't always seem to be "good results." God's work isn't always evident. We struggle because we remember the time we obeyed, yet things got worse. We remember the time when obedience brought other people's disapproval. We remember the time when obedience didn't correct the problem. Our heart cries out, "Danger! Rough road! Detour ahead! Insecurity!"

Interestingly, if we feel unsettled, wondering how obedience will impact us, we're really believing our limited knowledge, experience, and motives are better than God's. When we acknowledge our limitations in knowing the truth, we wonder why we'd ever disobey. God knows everything, created our ability to "experience," and is motivated by love and goodness. Why, in the world, would we ever disobey?

- When you realize you're hesitant to obey God, to what do you attribute your hesitation?
  o When you want to obey God, to what do you attribute your willingness?

I wonder if Sarah and Lydia, the objects of this lesson, ever considered their own limited understanding. We'll look into their lives and see some challenges all women—and people—face. Let's see what we can learn.

Sarah

A lot of Sarah's story is contained in the book of Genesis. She is a prominent character in God's beginning story of the Israelites, the future Jews. She and her husband, Abraham, face many challenges to their faith and trust in God. And like all of us, they have a mixed bag of motives, reactions, and results. But God knew everything from creation, and he still chose this unlikely couple to begin a mighty people and nation.

- Read Genesis 16:1-16, 18:9-15, 21:1-12. Abram and Sarai waited many years for God's promise to be fulfilled, but Sarai remained childless. How do you think they felt, especially since Sarai, being childless, was like a curse in their culture?
  o Have you ever had similar feelings waiting for God to take action on your behalf?
- If Sarai thought her barrenness was her fault, she may have felt guilty. If so, how do you think guilt contributed to her plan (16:1-6)?
- What results did Sarai's plan produce:
  o between Sarai and *Hagar* (vv. 4, 6):
  o between Sari and *Abram* (v. 5):
  o between future generations (vs. 11-12, 15-16):

- How have you seen disobedience toward God's plan bring difficult results, both personally or in others?

Giving a maid to the husband to produce children is acceptable, even valued, in Sarai's culture in order to remove the shame of the barren wife and provide progeny. Society actively belittles such a woman, and without the knowledge we have, they always assumed the woman was at fault. There is something wrong with her at the level of her worth and value. Any children born to the maid are considered the father's rightful heir, just as if the wife had borne them.

This practice is acceptable to people but not God. He knows and had already told Abram what he intends to do. But like all of us, if the promise isn't fulfilled in our expected timing or method, we take matters into our own hands. We can mistakenly believe God needs help, or maybe we didn't hear right. We get nervous and impatient. Our faith lags, and our trust falters.

God in his graciousness doesn't hate us for our reaction. Rather, God's mercy upon Abram and Sarai beautifully illustrates how he never gives up on us. In fact, he knew all about their sin before the beginning of time. Even though Abram and Sarai disobey God, he still pursues his original plan through them. He also changes their names to Abraham meaning "father of many" and Sarah meaning "princess."

- Abraham laughs at the thought of producing a son at ninety-nine years of age (Genesis 17:17), and then Sarah laughs at the idea (18:12). Why do you think they laughed?
  o Do you feel comfortable expressing all your emotional pain and pleasure to the Lord—even when you're laughing in disbelief?
  o Have you ever laughed at some promise or idea God gave you or communicated in Scripture? What happened in your situation?

Who are we kidding when we laugh in disbelief, thinking we are hiding from God? Doesn't he know everything? Isn't he right with us wherever we are? Doesn't he know our every emotion and know every motive of our hearts? Yet, shame, confusion, or pride can motivate us to try to hide. Hiding goes all the way back to the Garden of Eden. Adam and Eve's first response after sinning was to cover themselves and hide. The first cover-up! Abram and Sarai are only continuing a seemingly good response, which never worked. And never will.

- What finally happens for Abraham and Sarah (Genesis 21:1-2)? Why?
  o How does Sarah's laugh of disbelief turn into a laugh of joy (vv. 6-7)?
- Even though Abraham and Sarah didn't fully cooperate with God, why do you think he fulfilled his plan through them anyway?

God is gracious, merciful, and creative. When we fail or stumble, he still is glorified because then his grace, mercy, and creativity are featured. Of course, we shouldn't disobey on purpose. There are plenty of opportunities to disobey without hardly trying or planning!

In the case of Abraham and Sarah, the waiting until they were very old made God's miracle even greater. Anyone who knew them must have laughed too—in wonderment and shock. If they had become pregnant early in the story, God's glory wouldn't have been as easily acknowledged and people wouldn't have been as amazed. God knows how to bring glory to his name!

- Sarah is part of the "Hall of Faith" passage in Hebrews 11:11. What does this say about God's grace?
  o Why did he include her?

o What encouragement does the story of Sarah give you when you don't completely understand or are tempted to disobey God's plan?

Lydia

Lydia's city, Philippi, was a very important city in Macedonia (northern Greece today). The Philippian church began with Lydia during Paul's visit about AD 50-51. And, of course, Paul's epistle to the Philippians is to the believers there. Lydia cooperated with the Holy Spirit's wooing but had no possible idea of God's grand and mighty plan.

Lydia came to Philippi from Thyatira, which is famous for its dyes. A husband isn't mentioned, and she is a successful businesswoman. Maybe she's single or widowed.

- Read Acts 16:11-15. Luke and Paul arrive in Philippi and share the gospel with a group of women. What do verses 13 and 14 tell us about Lydia?

Since "worshipers of God" are meeting at the river outside the city for a prayer meeting, there aren't enough male Jews or converted Gentile men to form a synagogue since ten were required.

A seller of purple cloth was usually wealthy and a prominent citizen because purple cloth is a very expensive item, often worn as an indication of royalty. Such cloth was colored by a dye derived from the blood or juice of a shellfish called "purple of the sea" or "sea purple" and is referred to as *chalson* in Deuteronomy 33:19.

- Why was Lydia receptive to their message (Acts 16:14)?
- How was Lydia's family affected by her faith and obedience (v. 15)?

- How does she use her possessions to honor God (v. 15)?
- How would you describe Lydia's overall attitude toward God?

God wants to use anything we are willing to offer him. He designed Lydia to be successful before she ever acknowledged he had a plan for her. Her good works didn't save her, but they were the fruits of her faith.

Sometimes it's hard for us to remember there are people who have never heard the name Jesus even today. But the majority of people Paul and other missionaries met in their travels had never heard of him. Lydia was a "worshiper of God," which meant she had been converted to Judaism. Possibly the news about the strange things like Jesus' miracles and resurrection could have spread to other countries and to her. People could have traveled and shared the amazing events. But for someone to change his or her whole life based on some seemingly "foreign" kind of information, even if Jewish-related, is difficult. Such a commitment shows us the Holy Spirit is the one who draws hearts.

- When Paul wrote his letter to the Philippian church, he most likely had Lydia in mind as one of the believers he thanked God for (Philippians 1:3, 8). If you have ever struggled to obey God, how does Philippians 1:6 give you:
  o *comfort*:
  o *confidence*:
  o desire to obey *God*:

When Lydia responds to Paul's message about Jesus, she could never have known all God would do because she believes. She's the first of many to respond to the gospel.

Likewise, we can never imagine what God has in mind because of our obedience. He certainly doesn't *need* us to have his plans accomplished, but he wants to include us in his exciting grand plan. Even if Lydia had not cooperated with the Spirit opening her heart, the Holy Spirit would have worked through others.

In the rest of Acts 16, Luke gives examples of two others who become a part of the early church and its success in Philippi: a demon-possessed slave girl (vv. 16-18) and a jailer (vv. 27-30). God uses a variety of people: someone prominent, someone sick, and a working-class man. He is so creative, and his will is always for a person's good and his own glory. We all have an invitation and opportunity to be a part of his amazing world-domination plan. We may be more motivated to obey God when we remember God wants to include us in that plan.

- In Philippians 1:9-11, Paul talks about four specific ways to obey God. Express either in general and/or personal terms what each of these mean:
  o love may *abound* still more and more in knowledge and depth of insight:
  o discern what is best:
  o be pure and *blameless*:
  o be filled with *the* fruit of righteousness:
- In which of those four areas would you like your obedience to grow?
- What is the end result of obedience (Philippians 1:11)?
- Has God ever opened your heart to respond to the good news about Jesus' love for you and his death on your behalf, like he did for Lydia?
  o If so, what happened?

If not, would you like to ask Jesus to forgive your sins and become the Lord and Master of your life? Here is a suggested prayer of salvation.

These are just words, though, unless they come from your repentant heart.

Heavenly Father God, thank you for loving me so much that you sent your Son, Jesus, to die for my sins and rise from the dead. I acknowledge I am a sinner and repent of my sins. I need your love and forgiveness. I ask you to come into my heart and life to be my Lord and my Savior. Thank you for saving me and forgiving me. Amen.

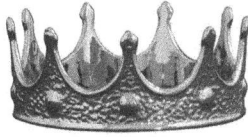

My precious Princess and Daughter:

I love you!

I know obedience is difficult sometimes. You have strong desires. But I know what I'm doing. You may have trouble trusting me at times. You may be unwilling to accept my plan. But let me assure you, I am always faithful in doing what is right and good. Though my request for your obedience may seem hard at times, I know the plan for your life I'm developing.

When circumstances seem too challenging to do what I say, just remember my Son, Jesus', obedience. Yes, even he felt challenged to obey in the garden of Gethsemane, so I understand what you're going through. But his obedience bought your salvation. Where would you be, and what would you be, without his sacrificial death and the empowering of my Spirit?

Focus on my nature. I am all-wise, powerful, kind, forgiving, and merciful. I desire only good for my children. You can obey me with confidence.

You will never regret putting my will first. Keep my commandments. Love me with all your heart, mind, and soul. Then you will see my power move through you. You will never regret obeying me.

Lovingly,

Your heavenly Father, the King

Lesson 7

Sapphira and the Samaritan Woman
Choosing Honesty

Little white lies. Fibs. Clouding the truth. Selective memory. We can call dishonesty by other names, but this kind of disobedience all boils down to something God hates. We try to tell ourselves lying is no big deal or the truth hurts too much. After all, if someone asks how their clothes make them look, are we supposed to tell the truth? They might be destroyed—or at the least discouraged. Then we would feel terrible.

We can be tempted to do anything to protect ourselves from pain, like not wanting to seem mean giving a friend the bad news about her appearance. Such "fibs" might not be so much about her feelings but about how we are perceived as mean (and then talked about!).

There are so many ways we can lie to ourselves. Self-deception is a strong temptation. And somehow we expect such lies will avoid pain. But usually, they only delay the consequences because dishonesty affects us more than we realize. Eventually, our wrong choices will be revealed and possibly be expressed in extreme, destructive behavior.

- What are some rationalizations and motivations people use for not telling the truth (or for only telling part of the truth)?

The Bible addresses dishonesty a lot, which is not surprising since God is truth and always tells the truth. And he uses characters from his Word to point out truth to us. Such is the case with Sapphira and the Samaritan woman. We can learn from both in different ways. Let's look at them now.

Sapphira

Sapphira and her husband, Ananias, are early believers in the newly created church. We actually don't know much about them, but evidently they are fairly well-off since they own property. Since they are able to reap a profit, they had somewhere else to live.

- Read Acts 2:42-47, 4:32-5:11. How do the Christians of the early church show their dedication to the Lord?
  o Do these acts seem to be voluntary or required?
- What do Sapphira and her husband do (5:1-2)?
- How is the story of Joseph in Acts 4:36-37 significant for Ananias and Sapphira's story?
- Why do you think the couple is dishonest?

Because there's no indication the selflessness and generosity going on in the church is required, the only possible motivation seems to be their oneness of heart and soul. They are grateful for what Jesus has done in their lives, having set them free from the bondage of sin. And they trust in God's provision for their future. What a witness to the unbelievers of the city.

The heart and soul are where our motives originate. Unfortunately, our motives for doing something right or wrong, including whether we lie, can be muddled within our hearts. We can easily convince ourselves our intentions are honest or our dishonesty is for the best. Sapphira and her husband seem to be motivated by being admired by their peers.

Significantly in Acts 4:36-37, Joseph's example (also known as Barnabas) of generosity and sacrifice comes right before the story of Ananias and Sapphira. Remembering there weren't any chapter divisions in the original writings of the Bible, we can see how Luke may be contrasting the righteous choice of one man and the unrighteous choices of a couple. He also could be indicating not everyone or everything was perfect in this community. And certainly none of us attend the perfect church, and we'll never find the perfect group of people.

- What significance do you see in Peter saying they had lied to the Holy Spirit instead of to him personally (Acts 5:3-4)?

Importantly, Peter didn't make this couple's lying about himself. Most of us would have taken their behavior personally. We would have been angry, bitter, or believed the lie this couple's bad behavior said something about the quality of the teaching they were receiving and who taught. Peter could have heard the "message" as "our teaching isn't good enough, clear enough, powerful enough"—or whatever a teacher or pastor or friend thinks is important for his or her own image.

But the truth is every person makes his or her own choices. This couple was selfish. They must not have trusted in God to provide for them, or they put too much stock in their possessions or wealth. They tried to cover all the bases, both their image and their own provision.

- Did Sapphira and Ananias sin because they gave only some of the money or because they lied about what they'd done?

Kathy Collard Miller

o What happened to Ananias (Acts 5:5)?

There was nothing wrong with keeping some of the proceeds of the sale for themselves. There was no rule saying they had to donate any or all their profits. Their sin was in lying about their choice to make themselves look good. Everyone else was giving all, so if they didn't, they might have feared criticism or losing status.

- What does Peter give Sapphira an opportunity to do (Acts 5:8)?
  o How does she fail the test?

Peter is a wonderful example of grace. He doesn't jump to conclusions. He doesn't condemn. He listens and seeks God's discernment. He can't know a person's heart motives without the Holy Spirit's instruction. And God seems to have given him an extra measure of discernment to know the truth and to declare God's judgement.

- What consequence does she suffer (Acts 5:10)?
- Why do you think God exacted such extreme consequences?
  o Why was this needed in the young Christian church?
  o What was the result of Sapphira and Ananias' discipline (v. 11)?

If God hadn't brought such a steep consequence, the other believers might think they could easily get away with dishonesty or other ungodly choices. Today, we can't always see the direct result of our own ungodly choices and the consequences God gives. At times, we don't even want to see the connection. But they are there because God knows sin and poor choices aren't good for us, and God wants only our best and good. God doesn't give those consequences to punish us but to train us in righteousness like he did in the early church.

- What lesson do you think God wants to carry from Sapphira into today's church?

The Samaritan Woman

The culture in the day when the Samaritan woman lived forbade men from speaking to women in public, Jews from dealing with Samaritans, and anyone from speaking to strangers. The woman we'll study now had three strikes against her in this society: she was a woman, a Samaritan, *and* a sinner. Nothing could have made the situation more unlikely for Jesus to pay attention to her and actually go out of his way to reach out to her.

- Read John 4:1-42. What emotions do you think the Samaritan woman felt when Jesus first spoke to her (vv. 7-9)?

Even though this woman is considered a sinful outcast, God views her differently. Because she is important enough to Jesus, he "had to pass through Samaria." Actually, he didn't *have* to. No other Jew did. They avoided that area at all costs—even at the cost of taking the longer route around Samaria. The Jews hated the Samaritans and avoided them like the plague.

Judea is located in the south of Israel and Galilee is in the north. In between is Samaria. To the east of Judea is Perea, and this is where Jews walked to reach Galilee—around Samaria! In other words, every Jew took more energy and time than needed in order to avoid the hated Samaritans.

The animosity between the Jews and the Samaritans goes back in history to the time of Ezra (Ezra 4). The original "Samaritans" had a mixed ethnicity, including a Jewish background. Because they were not pure in their breeding, the Jews looked down on them. As a result, the

Samaritans reciprocated by building their own temple and rejecting the Old Testament except for the Pentateuch (first five books of the Old Testament). They even claimed to have an older copy than the Jews. Over time, the antagonism between the two groups heightened until there was little contact. Of course, Jesus knew about all this and also discerned the motives within all the people over history who contributed to these dysfunctional societies. Regardless of the antagonism between these two groups, Samaritans were proud of their heritage. Since they were so hated, they tried to protect their image (or so they thought) by hating the Jews and taking pride in what they did have—the alternate temple and a connection to Jacob through the well. "Jacob's well" is supposed to be where Rachel gave Jacob water.

This Samaritan woman comes to get water at "the sixth hour," which commentators say could indicate noon or six in the evening—the hottest parts of the day. Regardless, most women arrive at the beginning of the day when the weather is cooler. With many there, they gather and gossip. Certainly, this needy woman is often the topic of their conversations because she's "bad."

We can't help but be convinced the "meeting" between this sinful woman and Jesus is orchestrated for her benefit—and ultimately the town's. The women who aren't there and have previously shown contempt for this woman would eventually be jealous they didn't have the privilege of having a private chat with Messiah Jesus, who exudes such love for the needy one. If you know Jesus as your Messiah, Lord, and Savior, you can have a private chat with him any moment in the day and receive an outpouring of love and understanding. What a precious gift.

In the following verses from John chapter 4, identify how Jesus directs the conversation and how the Samaritan woman grows in her spiritual understanding as she faces truth honestly.

Jesus	Samaritan Woman
7-8:	
9:	
10:	
11-12:	
13-14:	
15:	
16:	
17:	
17-18:	
19-20:	
21-24:	
25:	

Jesus asks her for a drink. He knows the "theme" of thirst he's choosing for her. By asking a question, rather than demanding, he's giving her power, and in life she rarely feels powerful. His question gives her the opportunity to choose whether to respond and grant his request. From the very first thing Jesus says to her, he is different from every man she's ever met, because every other man assumed he was in control and didn't ask her for anything—only demanded and expected full compliance.

After their discussion, during which he reveals himself as the Messiah, she has a heart change. She is convinced and convicted. He has revealed things only God could know. Jesus developed her thirst by:

- establishing an awareness of the need through curiosity and relating to the current situation (being at a well)
- offering hope
- confronting sin
- identifying himself as the solution.

Throughout the encounter, he doesn't take offense. He is gentle, yet undeterred. He doesn't get sidetracked. What an example for Christians in sharing the gospel message.

When she admits, "'I have no husband,'" in John 4:16, she isn't completely honest. Although her statement is true in the technical sense, because she's not legally married, he's really a live-in boyfriend. Therefore, she can skirt the issue and deny she has a husband.

But Jesus wants her to dig deeply. He knows her situation, of course, but by giving her the opportunity to lie, he is exposing her deceptive heart—and her need for a heart change. She may be seeing herself truthfully for the first time in the eyes of Jesus. Because he isn't responding with condemnation, his judgment is actually attractive to her. There's possibly a sense of hope within her for the first time, which Jesus will develop.

Chances are, her husbands became ex-husbands through a combination of divorce and death. But how isn't important to Jesus. He is interested in drawing her heart to himself, not every detail separating her from him. He calls any sin "sin." There are no levels. Her sin of adultery is not any more serious than when she has lied or gossiped. All of her sins separate her from him. Different sins may have greater or lesser consequences, but they all separate her—and us—from God.

- When the Samaritan woman honestly faces the truth, what does she learn about Jesus (John 4:25-26)?
- What truths about Christianity, God, or your lifestyle did you have to face honestly in order to believe in Jesus as your Savior? If you've never accepted Christ as Savior, what barriers do you face?
- How do we know the Samaritan woman actually faced herself truthfully (vv. 28-29)?

The woman's water pot in this story represents so much more than an object of hydrating her body. Going home without this essential "source" suggests she is extremely excited and enthusiastic as she is diverted from the original goal of being there. Her original thirst is overcome by the thrill of having her heart and soul refreshed. She doesn't need a temporal thirst quencher when her soul has been doused and satiated with living water.

Leaving behind the water pot is also a commitment she'll return to see Jesus. She isn't leaving to avoid him. She is concentrating now on other things. She leaves with the intention of sharing the good news she's just learned. She's actually concerned about the people who have rejected and condemned her.

Her heart is transformed, and she isn't afraid to speak about what she has encountered. Previously, she avoided people. Now she seeks them out because she has great news to share. And she's honest in referring to her sin by declaring Jesus told her all she ever did. Even the bad stuff. She doesn't try to cover up her sin with talking about the "balance" of all the good stuff. She is brutally honest

- What happens as a result of her honesty and openness with others (John 4:30, 39-42)?
- Have others come to know Jesus because of your own honesty and openness?
    o In what ways do you need to change so you can participate in reaping the harvest (vv. 35-38)?
    - What is even more important to Jesus than physical food (vv. 31-34)?
    - How did Jesus' doing his Father's work make an impact on the Samaritan woman's life?
    - Has Jesus' work made an impact in your life? If so, in what way?

- Read Exodus 1:15-21. Is lying always wrong?
  o Are there any areas of your life where exaggeration, little white lies, or dishonesty cloud your ability to live a godly life? Explain.
- What general commands about lying are given in Leviticus 19:11?
  o In Psalm 51:6:
  o In Zechariah 8:16:
  o In Colossians 3:9:
  o What do John 8:44 and John 16:13 say about lies and lying?
  • What do Sapphira and the Samaritan woman each teach you?

My precious Princess and Daughter:

I want you to be honest. Honest with others, with yourself—and with me. The temptation to lie or to be less than honest is strong, I know. Yet covering up sin or weakness attacks the very core of the security and significance all humans need and I meet. Lying says I don't meet those needs.

I made your needs so that you would need me. So that you would seek me for your security and significance. Not through exaggeration or little white lies making your story more attractive, making you feel more important, or preventing you from suffering the consequences of a poor choice.

Through my Spirit's power, you can choose honest communication and vulnerable sharing. If you admit your faults to others, their prayers for you will strengthen your ability to succeed in godliness.

Be honest. You need my help and others' help. That's the way I made it. You are designed and called to reflect me to the world around you, but no one will see me behind your lies. The choice is yours. But let me assure you, there are great blessings in being honest.

Lovingly,
Your heavenly Father, the King

Lesson 8

Bathsheba and Hannah
Dealing with Temptation

Temptation is no fun. Relationships can be destroyed. Businesses can be lost. Addictions can ruin families. There are innumerable ways to be tempted. Succumbing to any temptation is rooted in distrust of God.

We can easily wonder why life can't be free of choices offering sin. And to increase the risk, why do such opportunities seem so attractive? Doesn't seem fair.

Such temptations occur for every single person who has ever lived. Possibly, Christians are more aware of being tempted because we are more sensitive to the conviction of the Holy Spirit. Yet such awareness doesn't remove the struggle. We continue to reject his help.

No Christian is exempt, even those we see from afar and think they would never give in. They are human like us, and also experience mental anguish of failure. Yet, longingly, we hope we'll be able to rise above temptation.

Kathy Collard Miller

- How do you react when you recognize you're being tempted?
  o What area of temptation is the hardest for you to resist?

Bathsheba and Hannah both faced temptation, but in different areas of life. Their responses were different, too. Let's see what we can learn from them.

Bathsheba

When Bathsheba took her famous bath, she had no clue what would happen to her, her husband and the nation of Israel. Did she plan her little escapade? Did she know King David was in town? He was supposed to be out fighting, as her own husband was. How could she have known in those moments the king would be restless and meander on his roof? Do you wonder if she had taken other baths there, but nothing bad had happened? She couldn't have known this time would be different—and crucial. With *this* bath, everything changed with dire consequences.

We'll never know everything about this situation, but God does. He always knows the intentions and motives of every heart. He let the scenario play out, knowing how he would use their sin for his glory as a reflection of his sovereignty and his grace.

- Read II Samuel 11:1-27, 12:15-25. How did Bathsheba open herself up to temptation (11:2)?
  o Do you think there was any intention on Bathsheba's part to get David's attention? Explain your answer.

Although this passage is written with an emphasis on David, Bathsheba bears responsibility for her part in the adultery. David and Bathsheba's sin potentially could bring more destruction than they ever imagined. God had already determined the future eternal King, his

Son, Jesus, would come through the line of David. Although God can sovereignly make sure his will is done, the repercussions of sin almost destroyed David's legacy.

When we are tempted to sin, we do well to remind ourselves the effects of disobedience might seem minimal since we can only see the temporal consequences. Small, sinful choices can add up to huge consequences.

God chose to bring good from this sin in the form of his Son through an ungodly line of ancestors. How like him to be gracious to fulfill his plan.

- What part do you think Bathsheba is responsible for?
- What other options do you think she had?
  o before she bathes on the roof:
  o when David sends for her:
  o when she realizes *what* David's intentions are:
  o when she identifies her *pregnancy*:

Although it is customary for women to bathe in their courtyards, they would be protected by the walled enclosure. But, of course, the palace was higher, which allowed the king to see below (something she surely would have known).

When David calls for her, and she understands what he wants, she's in a very dangerous situation. To refuse a king is a possible death sentence. Yet, when we are tempted, and there seem to be no other options, God will provide solutions if we look to him.

We know Bathsheba's baby was not from her husband, Uriah, because the purpose of her bath was to become cleansed after her menstruation was done, as the Law commanded (Leviticus 15:19). Therefore, she isn't already pregnant when David calls for her.

Comment briefly about how a woman can handle temptation in each of these situations:

- o A man at work suggests she go out to dinner with him, and she's married.
- o Someone offers her a fatty dish or desert, and she's trying to lose weight.
- o She's talking to *someone* about a mutual friend who is struggling with sin, and she's tempted to pass the information along as a "prayer request."
- o She's tempted to *exaggerate* a story to increase the entertainment value.
- • What lies have you recognized as coming from Satan when he's trying to convince you to give in to temptation?

Satan is very clever and creative. His tempting lies can include an assortment of ideas. Since he knows our weaknesses, he fashions them according to our struggles. He could say:

- o *Oh, it's no big deal. Just this once won't hurt anything.*
- o *God doesn't want you to miss out on* something *you value. He loves you.*
- o *God's* command *doesn't apply to this particular situation.*
- o *Well, you've already sinned a little, so you might as well continue. Everything's hopeless anyway.*
- • Or what is his most common lie for you?
- • What is Satan's most common strategy (Revelation 10:12)?
- • According to Revelation 10:12, what gives you power to resist his lies?

- As a result of the adultery, David arranges for Bathsheba's husband, Uriah, to be killed (11:6-25). If Bathsheba had known of this plan, what could she have done or said to prevent this further sin from happening?
- Bathsheba took a bath openly exposed, slept with a man other than her husband, and married the man who had her husband murdered, yet she became the mother of Solomon and part of the bloodline of Christ. How does God's work speak to you?
- How does Solomon's birth represent God's grace and forgiveness (II Samuel 12:24-25)?

Hannah

Hannah is a broken-hearted woman, who only wants to have children. When she can't conceive, she's considered inferior both by her husband's other wife and society. As a barren woman, she's blamed for not conceiving. The townspeople believed she doesn't have God's favor or blessing, and God must have put a curse upon her. To make matters worse, her husband's second wife, Peninnah, makes Hannah's insecurity count in her own favor.

- Read I Samuel 1. What irritation and pain did Hannah constantly face (vv. 6-7)?
  o How did she relieve the pain (v. 7)?
  o What temptation(s) did Hannah face in her reaction to Peninnah?

Elkanah's family suffers the consequences of polygamy. Such a choice isn't approved by God and also shows a lack of trust in God. Many times polygamy is a man's self-effort to provide children through a second wife when his wife is barren or a selfish way to have more children, giving him status in society. The more wives, the more children, the greater admiration.

Another reason? The more children, the more help the father receives in the fields or another line of work. These might all seem reasonable in the world's eyes, but as Hannah's example shows, relationships are affected. Only God's design for marriage and the family is best.

- Elkanah tries to comfort Hannah. Do you think his words were soothing (I Samuel 1:5, 8)?
  - How do you think his *words* made her feel?
  - What do you think she wanted to hear from him?
  - Why do you think Hannah was not able to receive the devotion her husband offered her?
- Have you rejected someone's love? Why?
  - What do you want to hear from others when you are struggling with pain or temptation?
  - What words could you say to communicate your need for help?

Ultimately, no one can provide what we need. Our husband may not know the right words, because, as a man, he looks at things differently. His attitude most likely will be similar to Elkanah's *I should be enough. Don't feel like this.* Unfortunately, when husbands or men try to deal with a woman's emotions, they feel helpless. They don't understand the "drama" and can get irritated because they feel powerless and can't seem to make things better. The more they love their wife, the more they can feel incapable. And few men like to feel incapable and powerless because God designed them to be the warrior and protector!

Unfortunately, we might interpret their frustration as meaning we aren't loved and cared for. A vicious cycle of misunderstandings and hurt feelings begins. Maybe Hannah is caught up in such a scenario. Satan might be accusing her of being unlovable, both by her husband

and God. Yet God wants her to believe the truth: he loves her and cares about her pain. In time, he would show her his love and favor.

- Hannah prays and weeps before the Lord, but she still experiences "bitterness of soul." How can both be part of a godly response (I Samuel 1:10-11)?
  o How did Hannah handle her grief? Do you think she was tempted to blame God, her husband, or herself? Or any combination?
- Do you think it's OK to express your feelings to God, even if they are angry feelings?

We can easily try to hide our feelings from both others and God. We may feel ashamed to have "negative" feelings. Those feelings may seem like we aren't trusting God. And certainly it's possible these feelings stem from distrust of God, but they don't always. Hannah gives us the godly example. She expresses her grief to God, trusting he will do the right thing for her.

- Eli's misunderstanding of Hannah could have been a temptation for her to react in a hostile way (I Samuel 1:12-14). Instead, what does she choose (vv. 15-16)?
- How do you feel when you are misunderstood?
  o What are some negative and positive ways to respond to misunderstandings?

Quite often, when we feel misunderstood, we can hear Satan whisper his "messages" in our minds and our hearts:

   o *I'm* insignificant *because the other* person *isn't really paying attention.*
   o *I'm stupid* because *the other person must believe what I'm saying isn't very intelligent.*

- *I'm a liar because the other person* must *believe I'm not telling the truth.*
- What is the message you sometimes hear? What is the truth of what God says about you? (If you need help with this, check out Ephesians 1.)
- If you feel misunderstood by God, why? Again, what is the truth?
- Another temptation Hannah faced was whether to believe God's prophet (I Samuel 1:17).
  o What do her facial *expression* and emotional attitude indicate (v. 18)?

Since Hannah had not told Eli what she was praying about, she might have thought, *How can he say what will happen when he doesn't even know what I asked of God?* Instead, she accepts his message as one from God. She may have trusted him as a priest and prophet who must be in tune with God. She may have felt understood for the first time, which certainly speaks of a God who knows—and understands—everything. And certainly she wanted to believe Eli's "promise" was God's promise.

But sometimes we feel more insecure as we wonder if we're hearing God correctly. We're afraid our own desires and motives are interpreting the message in the way we want. We may feel tense, but God knows our hearts. If we truly surrender to what he wants for us, we can trust he'll fulfill his will.

- What happens to Hannah (I Samuel 1:19-20)?
- What is Hannah's vow in verse 11?
- Hannah must have been tempted to go back on her vow. After all, she might not have any more children. But what does she do (vv. 21-28)?
  o What additional blessing does Hannah receive from the Lord

(2:21)?

    o What additional temptation might she have faced now (especially in relation to Peninnah)?

- Compare the consequences Bathsheba received and Hannah is rewarded with.

    o *Bathsheba's* actions and consequences:

    o *Hannah's* actions and consequences:

- Although resisting temptation doesn't guarantee only good things will happen to you, what benefits do you think you will see regardless?
- Read I Corinthians 10:13. What insights does this give you?
- Read Hebrews 4:14-16. What do these verses tell you?
- What specific step can you take to strengthen yourself against the next temptation in the area you mentioned in the first question of this lesson?

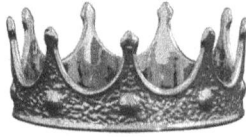

My precious Princess and Daughter:

I don't blame you for feeling tempted. Sometimes a temptation may seem overwhelming. Just think of my Son, who was tempted in similar ways as you. He was able to resist, because he trusted my plan, knew my words, and wanted my purposes fulfilled.

I know my plans, words, and purposes are best for you also. The tempter is my enemy, and he tries to hurt me by hurting you and offering you ways to disobey or ignore me. When the tempter comes along and tries to convince you he has a better plan, remember my strength and wisdom are available to you. My manual, your Bible, lets you know my will. Study my love letter to you and trust I have a better way.

Your uniquely designed path may take you through valleys and shadows, but ultimately you'll be glorified with me in heaven. I'm not finished with you until then.

In the meantime, call upon my strength. You can resist through my Spirit. But the choice is yours.

Lovingly,

Your heavenly Father, the King

Lesson 9

Miriam and Leah
Struggling with Jealousy and Discontent

Add to jealousy, envy. To envy, comparisons. What do you get? Discontent. How easily we can fall prey to these enemies of godly living! The lie "the grass is always greener on the other side of the fence" lures us to think other people lead perfect—or near perfect—lives, and we just need to get our act together. Or someone else needs to get their act together! But as someone has said, "The grass on the other side of the fence is Astroturf!" All fake! There's no such thing as "greenest," because everyone has difficulties and challenges.

Another lie is: "if only …" which snatches our affections away from Christ. If only my husband would say he loves me more. If only my church would meet my needs. If only my boss would give me credit. If only my coworker wouldn't lie about me. If only … If only … There are so many possible scenarios. How easily and quickly we succumb to the lure of jealousy, envy, comparisons, and discontentment.

- What things or opportunities belonging to other people are the hardest for you to do without?

  o How do you feel when you think of your lack in those areas?

In this lesson, we'll look at two women, Miriam and Leah, who struggled with these very things. Let's be assured we are never alone, and we're not the only ones facing these temptations. And most of all, we can know God cares and wants to strengthen us to find our contentment in him.

Miriam

Miriam is the sister of Moses. You know, the one who follows her baby brother as he floats down the river in a basket and then tells the princess she knows of a woman who can nurse him. From the beginning, this girl, who becomes a leader among the Israelites, has smarts and courage.

Stop and think for a moment how dangerous encountering the princess could actually be. There is every possibility the princess will understand what is going on—and the young girl will be a target. But, she loves her brother and wants the best for him, motivating her courage to risk all.

Unfortunately, Miriam isn't without her struggles as time passes. She succumbs to jealousy, envy, and discontentment. During the Exodus, most likely Miriam is in her nineties, Moses is eighty, and Aaron is eighty-three. Obviously, God uses even those in their older years.

- Read Exodus 15:20-21. Miriam is sister to both Moses and his older brother Aaron. When we first see Miriam as an adult, what is she doing?

- Read *Numbers* 12. When we next see Miriam, what is she doing (vv. 1-3)?

  o What seems to be the root of her jealousy (vv. 1-2)?

  o Do you *think* Moses deserved her criticism (vv. 3, 7-8)?

- Have you ever experienced feelings similar to Miriam's? Explain your answer.

Jealousy, criticism, and discontent all run together in the club called disobedience. They feed and encourage each other to distrust God. At the time, such feelings and choices seem absolutely reasonable and acceptable. We are caught in a web of justification and self-pity. The motive might come from any number of sources: insecurity, attacks from Satan, childhood wounds, being told we are "less than," believing we'll never measure up and/or feeling hopeless and depressed. Jealousy and envy can start small and blossom into a huge weed. Thankfully, God's Spirit wants to come to our aid and empower us to remember who we are "in Christ," and he doesn't compare us to anyone. What great news—the news of the gospel.

- How does God respond to their jealousy (Numbers 12:4-8)?
- How does God discipline Miriam (vv. 9-10)?
- Have you experienced God's discipline as a result of your jealousy, envy, or discontentment? How?

Although Miriam's discipline may seem extreme, the fact is jealousy, envy, and a critical spirit all belittle and demean God's holy name. Those ungodly reactions say God is mean-spirited, and he's withholding something good. They say he favors some people, and he's unfair. They say he isn't wise because what he's doing isn't right. We can easily forget the ungodly choices we make say something negative and untrue about our perfect, great, and good God. Then his name isn't glorified.

- Why do you think Aaron doesn't also get leprosy?

Although commentators and theologians can't say for sure, there are a variety of opinions on why Aaron didn't also get leprosy. For one, Miriam was the instigator of criticizing Moses. Although unclear from Numbers 12:1, in the Bible someone being named first indicates he or she is the primary person in the story. Every other time the Bible mentions Miriam and Aaron, Aaron is listed first, because he is the firstborn male in the family, and the family inheritance would go to him. Additionally, the Hebrew verb used in Numbers 12:1 for "speak" or "spoke" is in the feminine singular indicating Miriam did the speaking.

A possible second reason is Aaron is the high priest and therefore is needed to ask forgiveness for himself and his sister. If he also had leprosy, he would be considered unclean and therefore unable to approach Moses to ask him to intercede.

Another commentator suggested a third possibility. As high priest, Aaron has a tender heart, a gift from God, so that he can care about the people and intercede for them. Seeing his sister whom he loves having such a difficult disease would actually be more painful to him than if he had received the same consequence. God often gives people different consequences and disciplines them in different ways, because what one person values might not be what is meaningful to another. Similarly, we respond uniquely to each of our children. What motivates one toward future obedience won't motivate another.

Of course, we don't know if these possibilities are reality, but trusting God knows best is the best reason for us to be at peace with God's seemingly unfair reaction.

- How does Aaron change his attitude (Numbers 12:11-12)? Do you think Miriam did the same?

- Based on James 5:16, how does this principle of confessing our sins (like jealousy, envy, and discontent) act as a deterrent to future temptations?
  o In the confession and asking for forgiveness for jealousy, how would we be "healed"?

Healing might be having the strength to release the hold of lies that foster jealousy, envy, and discontent. We could release feeling God is treating us unfairly and not giving us what we deserve. We could be healed to be able to say, *Not my will, but thine, Lord*. Or we could forgive those who have hurt us, especially if they have prevented us from gaining what we want.

- How does Moses' response show his goodness and humility (Numbers 12:13)?
- What is the final consequence Miriam experiences (vv. 14-15)?
- How do the people show their respect for Miriam (v. 15)?
- What lesson might God be teaching the children of Israel through Miriam's example?

Leah

Leah is a very needy woman who puts her sense of worth into her husband's hands. Most likely, from the very beginning, she is considered the inferior sister to her favored younger and beautiful sister, Rachel. Thus, jealousy, envy, and discontent are born in Leah's heart. Maybe she fantasizes how having a husband would propel her to a better status and make her feel loved. And as the older sister, society said she should have married first. We will soon see how her father, Laban's, trickery gains her a reluctant groom, leaving her fantasy unfulfilled. It'll take a long time for Leah to forsake her jealousy. Let's hope we don't take as long.

- Read Genesis 29:13-35. Describe briefly what happens.
- What do we know about Leah and Rachel from verse 17?
- What deceitful trick does Laban pull on Jacob (vv. 21-25)?
  o How do you think Leah feels about the deception?
  o Why do you think she goes along with the trickery?
  o How do you think Jacob's reaction to the switch makes Leah feel (vv. 25, 30)?
- How do you think Leah feels toward her sister Rachel?
- Leah obviously knows and agonizes over being unloved. What do the names she gives her children show (vv. 31-35)?
- What one thing does Leah want?
- When you feel discontent, are you focusing on God? If not, where is your focus?

Although God designed us females to want to be loved, he never intended for us to be totally fulfilled in other people's opinions of us or their level of love for us. Leah's total focus was on somehow getting her husband to love her no matter how many children it took. Her discontent was based in "someday." She must have thought, *Someday, Jacob will love me, and then I'll feel loved.* If we believe Satan's lie, we can succumb to jealousy, envy, and discontent. But we can guard our hearts with the truth.

- How does II Corinthians 10:5 teach us to believe the truth?
- Read Genesis 30:1-24. How does Rachel feel toward Leah?
- Can you think of other situations (biblical or contemporary) where two people are jealous of each other?

Jealousy can run the gamut from a slight annoyance to great consequences. Even murder can result. Husbands/boyfriends or wives/

girlfriends can become so jealous that they murder a rival. Jealousy can cloud our minds from the truth and result in actions we never thought we'd choose. We determine no one will make us feel inferior, inadequate, rejected, or unchosen.

Although envy and discontent are traits and reactions only experienced by humans, jealousy is a part of God's righteous nature, which may seem completely inappropriate. But his jealousy is motivated by love and goodness. Exodus 34:14 says *For you shall not worship any other god, for the LORD, whose name is Jealous, is a jealous God.* He doesn't want us to worship any other "god" because his love for us wants our best. Therefore, he will do whatever he can to try to convince us to worship and serve him only.

- What pattern do you see in Genesis 30:1-24?
  - o Describe the atmosphere you think existed within Jacob's home.
  - o No one seems to know what to do about the tension there. If you could advise those three adults, what would you tell them?
  - o How do you diffuse tension in your home?
- What conflict did the discovery of mandrakes produce (vv. 14-15)?
- What did Leah and Rachel's jealousy deteriorate into (vv. 15-16)?
- What part do you think Jacob played in the feelings between the two sisters?
- What do you think Jacob should have done?

Mandrakes were considered a fertility enhancer. When Reuben, Leah's son, who may have been around four or five years old at the time, gathered the plant with its fruit, Rachel found out. Instead of hoping in God, she looked to a plant to bring her the answer to her hopes, dreams, and prayers.

Whether something like a fertility enhancer is sinful is dependent upon our heart's motive. If we discard trust in God's plan, we're saying he doesn't know what is best. Interestingly, Leah's discontent focused on gaining what Rachel possessed—the love of Jacob—and Rachel's discontent focused on gaining what Leah possessed—many children. We want what we don't have and we don't appreciate what we do have because of jealousy, envy, and discontent.

Sadly, Rachel dies giving birth to her second son, Benjamin, which ironically is the very thing she thought would bring her contentment.

- Even though Leah struggles with jealousy, whom does she look to for comfort (Genesis 30:20)?
- What is Leah's constant hope (v. 20)?
- Jealousy, envy, and discontent are often like strong tentacles in our attitudes and choices. Although Miriam and Leah did not achieve complete success in destroying those attitudes, what can we learn from them?

Based on I Timothy 6:6-10, fill in the blanks:

> Godliness is best when accompanied by _____.
> When we die, we'll take _____ with us. We should
> be content if we have _____ and _____.
> Having money as your only goal can bring _____
> and _____. Money is not the root of all evil, because
> the Bible actually says, "the _____ of money is the
> root of all evil." It causes people to _____ and turn
> from the _____.

- How would you define someone who is rich?
- How do you think someone from a developing nation would define

a rich person?

o *What* makes the difference?

- From I Timothy 6:17-19, what instructions are given to the rich?

    o *verse* 17:

o *verse* 18:

o *verse* 19:

- In what ways can you grow in your ability to resist jealousy and envy?

    o Do you anticipate such growth will bring more contentment into your life? How?

My precious Princess and Daughter:

Yes, there is much in life to want. There are so many who appear to have gained so much of what the world offers. You look at them and wish you could live their lives. Jealousy, envy, and discontent are knocking at the door to the desires of your heart. Will you let them in? Or will you trust I know what you truly need to be fulfilled?

Don't compare yourself to others. I have a unique and different plan for each one of my children. I do not measure you based upon someone else. I have a singular focus of expecting only what I know you can accomplish.

No one understands you like I do. I have great expectations especially designed for you. Why allow other people's accomplishments to intimidate you? I've given you a unique goal only you can fulfill. Keep your eyes on me, not others.

You are one of my Daughters. And I have enough love to create a different plan for each of you. Do not look at your sisters. Trust my plan for you is best—and my plan for my other children would not work for you.

Lovingly,
Your heavenly Father, the King

Lesson 10

Martha and Mary
Practicing God's Presence

Life is a challenge. We long for peace and knowing God is helping us and is with us. But we're so easily distracted by responsibilities, problems, and people. Sometimes we think we'll only be at peace when we're in a "quiet time" or some other spiritual activity. Sometimes we think those spiritual times are the only way to sense God's presence. Or those moments are when God is most pleased with us—when we're doing something "super spiritual."

But the truth is, God promises to be with us every moment regardless of whether we sense him and regardless of what we're doing. We can "practice the presence of God" whether we're diapering our baby or driving the carpool or leading a high-stress corporate meeting. God is with us, and everything we do in obedience to him is serving him—not just the seemingly "spiritual" activities.

Yet, we can still judge ourselves inadequate in the "spiritual" department if we compare ourselves to others. Some women just seem to have a natural bent toward being aware of God's presence and easily choose to have a set-apart spiritual time. Others of us struggle. We're too hyper. We have too much to do. We can't concentrate. There always seem to be so many obstacles.

- Describe when and how you feel most harried about life, most calm, and most "spiritual."
  o Is serving others, especially visitors, a source of stress or joy for you?

The sisters, Martha and Mary, who are close friends to Jesus, can relate. They seem to have opposite personalities and preferences. We can learn from them about how to incorporate spirituality with service and every aspect of life.

Martha and Mary

Focus on Luke 10:38-42 for the following questions. Also, read John 11:1-44 and John 12:1-3 for background information.

- What basic and opposite personality traits do Martha and Mary have?
- What kind of attitude is exposed in Martha's question?
- How was Mary insensitive to Martha's concerns?

Knowing the differences in personalities can enhance relationships. There are numerous ways to identify personality or temperaments, but a basic one separates them into four categories. Here are a few generalities about those four:

- **Expressive:** highly values fun, is talkative and loves a lot of time with people.

- **Driver**: highly values control, likes to "tell" people what to do rather than ask questions and believes his/her decisions are always right.
- **Amiable**: highly values peace at any cost, is an effective mediator, is quiet and sees the positive in everyone and everything.
- **Analytical**: highly values perfection, is detail-oriented and a great organizer but second-guesses decisions.

If we don't understand God created different personalities for his purposes, we can easily:

- judge ourselves less than or the opposite, superior.
- be discontent with our own personality, because another personality seems more attractive or useful.
- intensely hate our personality's weaknesses and think "God made junk."
- judge another personality as inferior.

We must remember each of these temperaments have strengths and weaknesses. God intended the strengths to be used to serve him and the weaknesses to cause us to need him. We might not always appreciate God's design, but he knew exactly his purposes in creating you.

- How does Psalm 139:1-6, 13-16 confirm those truths?
- Why do you think Martha talks to Jesus rather than talking directly to Mary to assist her with the food (Luke 10:40)?
- Why do you think they had trouble communicating?
  o What would have been a constructive way to solve this problem?

There can be all sorts of blocks to good communication, and sometimes women have even more difficulty than men. Men, generally speaking, prefer to state the facts and not get emotionally involved. But women crave relationship, and if a friend seems to indicate the relationship is not important by not communicating, she can take offense and avoid or reject contact. Plus, each temperament communicates in a different way. Martha and Mary are definitely struggling in their relationship, and the stress of hosting Jesus, whom they want to please, creates more tension.

- Do you relate more to Martha or Mary?
- What can you imagine Jesus would have said to each of them? What advice would you give them?
- What did Jesus actually say about Martha's activity (Luke 10:41)?
- What distracts and worries you in the following areas?

Area	Distracted because:	Worried about:
Hospitality:		
Extended family:		
Friendships:		
Ministry to others:		
Children:		
Husband/Boyfriend:		

- What do you think Jesus meant by "but only one thing is necessary" (Luke 10:42)?

When Jesus said *But only one thing is necessary,* one possible meaning could be "Prepare one dish instead of many. Come listen to me." If true, he may have been suggesting her expectations were too high, and she was trying to perform for him instead of receiving his unconditional love. Of course, we are going to serve Jesus out of love for him, but maybe her motives included believing he wouldn't love her if she didn't perform. Or maybe she wanted to look like a good hostess before others. Those impure motives are what feed anger, discontent, and contentiousness. Obviously, her priorities were out of kilter.

We can do the same thing if we believe service always equals or communicates love. Whether for God or for others, we must know what the other person values. Jesus values her presence more than lots to eat.

- If you were to focus more fully on Jesus' perspective, would there need to be any changes in your attitude, worry, or distractions?
- What insight into Jesus' attitude toward women do you gain from Jesus' encouraging these two women to spend time in his presence?

In their culture, women were only servants. They weren't supposed to be with the men at all. But Jesus upset the cultural norms over and over again, valuing women just as much as men.

- Do you hear a harsh rebuke or a gentle suggestion in Jesus' reply to Martha (Luke 10:41-42)?
- Do you most often hear God's "voice" as rebuking or wooing?

How we hear God's voice in our hearts can indicate a lot. Maybe we were scolded more than praised. Maybe we grew up thinking we didn't deserve any praise, and we only expected to be reprimanded and not acknowledged for our efforts. Maybe currently we're in a hurtful or damaging relationship.

You might want to "try out" different tones as you speak Jesus' words aloud. What emotion does a soft and encouraging tone bring up inside you? Also, try to say Jesus' words with different words to communicate several possible meanings. Perhaps, "Oh, sweetie, please don't worry about making a lot. We'll be full after one of your delicious dishes. I'd rather you chose being at my feet like your sis has. Come and join us now. I love you even if we starve in your house."

- Do you think Jesus is saying Martha is wrong to serve or women shouldn't have company over? Explain your answer.
  o What did Jesus say is the better choice?
  o What benefits do you suppose Mary experiences at the feet of Jesus?
- What good qualities do you see in Martha?
- In Mary?
  o Which would you like to incorporate into your life from each woman?
- Focus on John 11:1-44 for the following questions. What kind of faith and dependence upon Jesus is demonstrated in the sisters' message to Jesus (v. 3)?
  o What actions do Martha and Mary each take (v. 20)?
  o Are these compatible with their personalities?
- Martha is assertive in talking to Jesus—to the point she almost seems to be rebuking him. Yet how is her faith also revealed (vv. 21-22)?
- Who does Martha believe Jesus to be (v. 27)?
- If Jesus asked you the same question of verses 25 and 26, how would you answer?

Mary's words to Jesus are the same as her sister's initial response (v. 32). They regard Jesus as both Messiah and as a friend with whom they can be honest in the sharing of their grief. Why do you think Jesus had to give a direct invitation to prompt Mary to come see him (vv. 28-31)?

- Throughout the Gospels, we often see Christ involving others in miracles. How does Jesus involve others in the making of this miracle (v. 39), and what do you think was his motive?

Jesus is not only a good teacher—he is an effective mentor. Stories abound in the Gospels about how he delegates responsibilities to others as a means of training and coaching them. He invites disciples and followers to stretch beyond their own skills or confidence so they depend upon his confidence and his power in them.

Even now, he is doing the same thing in our lives when he opens doors we don't feel we have enough faith to open, or are qualified or knowledgeable enough to handle. There can be any number of blocks and obstacles whispering lies and saying the Holy Spirit can't be strong enough in us to overcome. We can instead trust if he assigns us a task or responsibility, he empowers us to fulfill his desire. He's not ignorant of our inadequacies and weaknesses. Instead, he has every confidence his power in us is sufficient.

- Jesus indicates the sisters still don't believe fully what he can do, yet he fulfills his plan anyway (John 11:40). When your faith is weak, how is Jesus' response meaningful?
- With three words, Christ raises Lazarus from the dead. How do you imagine Martha and Mary feel as they see Lazarus walk toward them, most likely with a huge smile?
- Have you ever had similar feelings after seeing God solve a

problem in your life or do something you couldn't have imagined or designed? Describe what happened.

- Focus on John 12:1-3. This passage shows a scene similar to the one in Luke 10:38-42: Martha is serving, and Mary is at Jesus' feet. This time, though, there is something missing from the previous incident. Describe.
- What changes do you think have occurred in Martha's heart, maybe as a result of seeing what Jesus did for them?
- What lessons do you learn from Martha and Mary about finding a connection in your life between the practical and the spiritual?
- How can you practice God's presence while accomplishing God's work?

My precious Princess and Daughter:

I know your life is hectic. My Son faced the human obsession of busyness when he lived on earth. I didn't originally design life to be full of unfulfilled expectations and hurried running around. The garden of Eden's atmosphere was peaceful beyond belief.

But now, you face this problem, my Daughter. Whether through other people's demands or the ones you put on yourself, life seems like a treadmill run at high speed. Maybe even a rollercoaster.

I want to assure you your activity doesn't make you look better in my eyes. I love you without question and accept you as my own, regardless of your accomplishments—or lack of them. Yes, I do have specific things for you to accomplish, but they do not make me love you more. I already love you as much as I possibly can.

Whatever the pace of your life, turn to me at any time. I am available every single moment. Call out to me and ask for my help, comfort, wisdom, or anything you need. You don't need to have a formal quiet time to know I'm with you. I am with you constantly, and I promise never to forsake you or leave you.

Succeed in my Spirit's power, but take time first to confirm I've called you to an opportunity. Fulfill my plans with a pure heart of wanting my glory. Your choices must come from your heart.

Lovingly,

Your heavenly Father, the King